﹏ divine design ﹏
HOW YOU CREATED THE LIFE YOU ARE LIVING

Gail Kathleen Minogue

MOSLEY
PUBLISHING
GROUP

POST OFFICE BOX 586602
OCEANSIDE, CALIFORNIA 92058-6502
WWW.MOSLEYPUBLISHING.COM

Mosley Publishing Group
P.O. Box 586502
Oceanside, CA 92058-6502
www.mosleypublishing.com

Editing by Robert Juran
Cover and interior design by Bryn Best

ISBN 1-886185-50-6

1st printing, September 2001

Printed in The U.S.A.

❧ divine design ❧
HOW YOU CREATED THE LIFE YOU ARE LIVING

é⚜❧

This book is dedicated to my Mother,
Willa Carolyn whose Soul taught me much
about love and acceptance.

❧⚜

❧ TABLE OF CONTENTS ❧

❧ Preface ❧

Dear Reader,

I wrote this book to provide you with simple and usable techniques to help you get in touch again with your Divine plan. I have purposely avoided the technical aspects of Sacred Geometry so that it would be easy and fun to discover your own path. So many individuals are in pain, loneliness and anger because their lives have taken turns away from their authentic selves. We have abandoned ourselves. I want these writings to be a push toward the "real" you. You don't have to say to others, "I work in an office but I am really an artist." We need you to be you, the authentic you.

Saint Thomas Logian wrote, "If you bring forth that which is within you, what you bring forth will save you. If you do not bring forth that which is within you, what you do not bring forth will destroy you."

Do not be destroyed by what sits waiting to be activated in your life. No matter the age, as long as you are on this Earth, you are growing and have opportunities to fulfill your heart's desire. We need you.

Gail K. Minogue, 2001

๑ *Chapter 1* ๛

"In the Beginning...."

*"It is the secret of the world that all things subsist
and do not die, but only retire a little from sight
and afterwards return again...."— Emerson*

I believe it was Woody Allen who once said, "I'm not afraid of
dying. I just don't want to be there when it happens." Perhaps
there is much validity in his statement. We seem to live our lives
as if death were another event that will happen one day, but in
the meantime, we won't dwell on it very much. We can go about
our days concentrating on the activities that can keep our bodies
here on Earth. As we all know, though, and we have heard it said
many times over, we will not get out of here alive. On top of
that, we spend very little time here—at the maximum 105 to 120
years. Death of the physical body is certain. It's a matter of
when and how and can happen at any moment.

Knowing, however, that we have a finite amount of time on
this planet, isn't it both wise and prudent to view our time spent
here as an opportunity—an opportunity to grow, evolve, learn
and enhance our awareness. When we leave, we will take with us
only what we learned, nothing more. A funeral shroud has no
pockets. For all the great people who have gone before us, not
one was able to take any piece of their "stuff" with them. What

1

they were able to take was the information and awareness that was imprinted on their Souls.

This book is about the imprinting of the Soul and the process involved in planning each life BEFORE BIRTH and the carrying out of that plan while you are still in the physical body. If we can truly understand that each lifetime we spend here is thoughtfully orchestrated prior to birth, we can begin to see that the time here is very important for our personal growth. What if we were aware of our own individual plans? What if we knew that we had a special calling, a specific direction and our own personal time frames? What if we knew our talents from past lives as well as our shortcomings? How differently would we live our life—probably very differently.

Imagine going on a trip without knowing where we were going, the route we would take, the items we would pack and the directions to get there. We would probably think it very odd. Yet so many of us live our lives without knowing where we are going or how to get there, taking items along that we don't need to carry. We are born into a family as a tiny bundle of energy. We go to school, grow up, get a job and conform to society, family, tradition and general rules of the tribe. We forgot that we had a plan of our own all along.

From my experience in working with many thousands of individuals over the years, the biggest question posed to me is "What is my true work in this lifetime, what is my purpose?" This question looms large on the minds of everyone. It can feel like a haunting— a gnawing sense of not doing what we truly want to do or doing work that pays well but gives little soul-satisfaction, or even worse, doing work that pays poorly and gives little soul-satisfaction. By knowing your own plan, you can set up your life so that you can see clearly the path you chose to take as well as what you said you would accomplish in this lifetime. You can also connect with your own time frame and start to create the situations that will work best for you and incorporate them in your life BEFORE they are really needed, almost as if you are setting things up for their proper time. You can become more successful and happier by avoiding disappointment and frustration when you are aware of these monthly and yearly influences. You can look into the future and begin to acquire the disciplines you will need at that time.

❧ *Chapter 2* ❧

Let's Go Backwards in Time . . .

"It is a gift to be allowed to reincarnate." June Burke

Many years ago I began a study of various ancient laws based on numerical order. I found this numerical order extremely accurate and began to use it in everyday life. I found common patterns in all things and in all cultures. It did not matter which language was used, all cultures and traditions included the same numeric patterns. It became very clear to me that there is an order to the universe that was put in place by a higher intelligence and that all things are in this Divine Order—including us. It became clear to me that our lives are planned, mapped out, arranged, whatever you feel comfortable calling it. It also became clear to me that we just didn't land here to be born, grow up, go to work, grow old and die.

Each one of us has a unique plan, a blueprint that we created before we came in. This plan was lovingly and carefully put together so that we could gain the knowledge and wisdom for our Soul's growth while we are here. This plan is so important to the individual that without knowledge of it, the Soul may have a difficult task in fulfilling its true purpose. We have heard the expression "Your days are numbered." It is taken from the Bible.

It means you are marked, coded and numbered with a plan. It does not mean, as many believe, that you have just so many days to live. Another biblical expression, "Every hair on your head is counted," also refers to the same plan. Every thought you think, every action you take, and every emotion you feel is imprinted on the Soul and is "counted in." All of this information is recorded for the future planning of your life. Each lifetime, therefore, is extremely important and is always an opportunity for your Soul's growth.

How is this life planned? What process takes place for us? How did I land with this family? Did I really pick these people? If I did, why in heavens name would I put myself in this situation? The questions can go on forever to dispute the fact that you could have planned this life. But what if you did plan it? What if you set it up so well that you truly know deep in your Soul what you really want to do? My answer to that question is that you do! At a Soul level, you know what you would like to learn and you know what you would like to accomplish before you leave this life. It's the connection to this information that has been lost. For you to be at peace in your life, it is imperative that you regain this connection. Find the plan again. The Soul remembers it all and is longing to experience the plan it created.

Where is this plan? Where did it go? How can I regain it? The answer is very simple. *You hid it.* Where did you hide it? The answer again is very simple—right out in front. It is hidden in your name and in your date of birth. Within these two lie all the information you need to guide you through your life. Your name contains information on your past lives, your talents, your karma, your personality, your destiny and your hidden motivator. Your date of birth contains your major learning lesson for this life, or what some might call your life path. This tells you the path you chose. It is the main direction for your life. Your date of birth also contains your time frames.

By understanding your own personal time frames, you can learn when to hold, when to fold and when to walk away, as they say in the old card game. What happens to so many of us is that we start new endeavors in our lives at the wrong time, or we leave endeavors too early. Timing is everything, you have heard people say. It is true. You want to be right on time in your own life so that you can plan and allow the process to take place. So many of us wonder why things don't happen in the time that we think they should. If we look at our own plan, we can see that it wasn't the right time. We can get very discouraged if we think it should have happened this year when actually the best time in our own plan is in three years. Awareness of our own plan makes all the difference.

Many people think they should be successful at a certain age. Many people "bloom early," fade away and bloom again later in life. Others will bloom very late and their greatest success won't come until after 50 years. To understand this more clearly, it is important to always remember that YOU ARE ON YOUR OWN TIME FRAME. You are not to compare yourself with your neighbor, your best friend, your coworkers, your father or mother or anyone else. You are unique and different, and thank God for the difference. Be patient, be aware and know your own plan. You have certain things you said you would learn, and they may or may not be similar to those of your neighbor or family members. That is why you can have a set of sextuplets born on the same day and at the same time and yet each might be very different from the others. Their names tell the story. Each one has a different personality, karma, motivation and destiny from their names. Just think of the heartache that could be avoided if we knew our own plan and other people in our lives knew theirs. If we could just pay attention to our own life and live in accordance with what we need to accomplish and learn, we could eliminate a tremendous amount of judgment of others and ourselves.

In working with my clients, the question has come up many times concerning the length of time we spend here working on our blueprint. The answer to that question depends on what the Soul has set out for itself. Remember that throughout your entire life you are a Soul, a spark of the Divine Intelligence who created a body to encase itself so that you could experience growth while you are here learning on this Earth. Picture a car with you as its driver inside the car. You drive around in your car. This is similar to the body. In fact, many people think their cars are the extension of their bodies. We always know, though, that the car is not you. This is similar to the body. It is a vehicle to encapsulate the Soul so that it can maneuver on the Earth plane. If we misuse the body, mistreat it and abuse it, it will not last and it will leave prematurely, just the same as a mistreated car.

When you are finished learning, you will dissolve the physical body (we call that death or transition), dissolve the personality that you created and move on to other realms, taking with you, as was stated before, only what you learned. It is my belief from many of the ancient teachings that a lifetime is approximately 120 years. I believe, that if we choose, we can extend that longer, at least another 30 years to 150. It is actually four cycles of the number 30 to complete the original blueprint or plan. Unfortunately most of us think we would be living a long time if we reached 90. That, in my belief, is erroneous. We should be thinking of old age beginning at 90 rather than being thrilled that we lasted that long.

Now, not all Souls have set themselves up to live the full 120 years. Some Souls are here for just five minutes or five years. They may only need to be here for a brief moment. Perhaps there is a Karmic situation with the parents that needs to be resolved. There can be many scenarios arranged, depending on the preplanning. It is, however, generally speaking, a plan of 120 years. Many of us leave prematurely due to neglect or irresponsibility of the physical body through a negative lifestyle, a lack of awareness, or impatience creating accidents for ourselves or a disconnect from our own intuition that could protect us and keep us from harm's way. So when I say to people that they should plan on 120 years, they look at me as if I have stated the impossible.

Instead, we plan on retirement at 55, 60 or 65. *The Soul never came in here to retire.* Retirement is a man made term created for the convenience of the governmental policy during a certain period of our country's existence. It was deemed appropriate due to the political climate and problems of the 1930s. It is not, however, a life-enhancing program. Rather than thinking of retirement at a certain age, is it not more prudent to consider a change in our lifestyle to accommodate what we know we are truly here to learn? Perhaps a better word for retirement is "restructure." Each of us can restructure his or her life so that it is in line with our original plan. We are not here to be comfortable, to be rich, to be poor, to be happy, to be sad or to be entitled. We are here to grow and continue doing so until we leave. In modern times, retirement has become the goal of one's life. You say, how much money will I have for retirement? The good news is that we are here to grow, learn and be productive until the moment we leave. You might restructure your life many times and have several "careers."

I know a woman who took the California bar exam 12 times, passing it on the 12th try. She wanted to be a lawyer, so at the ripe young age of 55 she set out to do just that. She bought her first house at 63. Now, that is life enhancing. She is planning to be successful well into her eighties, and has no plans to retire at all. Go into nursing homes and see what happens when people have stopped circulating. I have a friend from Saudi Arabia who calls today's nursing homes "houses of death" because nobody comes out alive. He also wonders why we put our older citizens into such places. As we wake up to the fact that we never came into this lifetime to retire, we will extend our lives accordingly.

Fear sells, and we are being told that security for retirement should be created by a certain age in life. The implication being that one will be too sick, too weak or too useless to be able to take care of oneself past a certain age. Thoughts and the spoken word are very powerful. Say it enough times and it becomes reality. We are living the reality of our words. Security here in the man made world is an illusion. At any moment the rug can be pulled out from under you either through your job, your home value, your stocks, your inheritance, your health, you name it. Your security is within you and your Soul's plan. It is within your intuition, your knowing and the belief that you are connected to the Divine Intelligence and that you will always know the best thing for you to do. In short, you can trust yourself no matter what it looks like outside of you. The Bible tells you "The power within you is greater than *anything* outside of you." Believe it, remember it, practice it. Take responsibility for your own life, your body, your thoughts and your choices.

๛ *Chapter 3* ๛

The Process of Reincarnation

"Seek not water, seek thirst first" Rumi

What is the process of reincarnation? Do we even believe in it? Why do I recognize certain people and places as familiar? Did I know them before? Why are some things so easy for me and so very difficult for others? What is this all about, anyway? In order to explain this life, we have to go back in time before you got here.

When a Soul (you) is going to reincarnate, that Soul will have, for lack of a better word, a meeting with a grouping of advanced Souls for a planning session. I will call these advanced Souls "guides." These guides will work with you to put together a plan for the next life or incarnation. During this process you get to review the records of all of your prior lives. In these records—sometimes referred to as Akashic Records—lies all the information on everything you have ever done, said, created and thought. From this review you can see the imbalances created from these prior lives. Sometimes we have been too wild and crazy, in some lives we have been too constricted, sometimes we have lacked compassion, in other lives we have been too enabling.

It is all there for your review. That is exactly what you will do—you will review these records. The Soul in this review process decides what it wants to concentrate on learning in this about-to-be-entered life. It asks, where do I need to make corrections, balance out past mistakes, what do I want to try to accomplish, what type of personality do I want to create, what experiences from previous lives do I want to call upon to help me in this next new life. It is a very thorough review. From this you will set up your plan with the guidance of the Advanced Souls. Some of the Souls who are assisting you will reincarnate at the same time to be part of what we call, here on Earth, the family of origin—your brothers, sisters, parents etc. During the first 27 years of the Soul's life there will be many corrections made with these people. We literally try to balance out experiences from the past with these people. It is very important to remember that by agreement YOU CHOSE THESE PEOPLE. It is not an accident that you are with them. With them you will be able to create the proper experiences and situations that will help you to get started with your learning lesson.

Many people do not consider the idea that we choose our own parents. Impossible, we say. Yet it is true. You have been with them before, and if it is appropriate, you will probably be with them again. You have unfinished business with them in this lifetime. Many times situations are created so that you will be challenged to grow in a particular manner. For example, if my blueprint or plan designated that I would come into this incarnation with the idea that I would strengthen my will, then it is possible that I would be born into a family that would be very tough on me. In order to sustain myself in that type of environment, I would have to strengthen my willfulness in order to survive—hence my initiating, pioneering spirit and willpower would all be made stronger in this environment. If it were too easy, there would be no opportunity to strengthen my will. So you can see we are always at the right place to grow and balance out our karma.

Perhaps you have chosen a Life Path of change or to learn how to make change constructively and to experience freedom. You might then be born into a family situation where the parents move around regularly either through job changes or have many changes in the household. You would, again in this case, be forced to continuously adjust to change and to learn to do it in a constructive manner rather than a destructive manner.

ଭୟ

ᔥ *Chapter 4* ᕋ

How Is This Plan Set Up?

"You Return by Choice"-A Metaphysical Teaching

This plan is set up using vibrational forces of sound. The plan is cloaked in the sounds of numbers. Numbers are not just mathematical quantities. They are living, breathing vibrational forces. If you say numbers very, very slowly, you will hear the different sounds in each number. Notice how your lips move through the sounds, and notice the shape of your mouth as you make these sounds. It is through sounds that particles are moved in the universe. If we only knew how powerful our words are, we would be extremely careful in what we say. If we say something over and over, we literally can create a force field that creates that event or situation. We have heard it said, by your words you will be praised or condemned. We have also heard the expression "the rich get richer and the poor get poorer." This also has much to do with the words spoken by these two groups.

This force field of energy is also contained in the sounds of our names. The energy of our plan is in the sounds of our name and date of birth. How do we create the plan with the numbers? We create it through letters and the quantity of numbers behind each letter. For instance, if your name is Ann, the first letter is a 1 for "A" followed by 14 and another 14 for the two "n's". (N is the 14th letter of the alphabet). You know now that Ann is really 1, 14, and 14. Ann is numerically coded and marked by numbers and the sounds that are created by those numbers. If you have never thought about numbers being vibrating energy fields, think about all the expressions we use around numbers. The Bible is full of them, for example: it rained 40 days and 40 nights or he prayed 40 days and 40 nights, they wandered 40 years in the wilderness, they were in captivity 400 years, there were five vestal virgins, seven times around the wall of Jericho and on and on. What do these mean? Did somebody just make them up? Or how about our own jargon, "the whole nine yards" (not six or seven or eight), "the cat has nine lives", she was "dressed to the nine's," or he is "behind the eight ball"—why isn't he behind the six ball or the seven ball, why are there nine innings in a ball game? All of these signify specific meanings due to the real meaning behind the numbers rather than the quantity of the number. Numbers are symbols.

As you work with your guides in putting together your own individual program, you will create a name that best suits what you would like to work on in the next incarnation. Your guides will name you. You are also in agreement with this arrangement. But you say, I hate my name. I would never choose this name. Better yet, you say, I was named after my father or Aunt Sue, etc. No, you named yourself. This name of yours, chosen before birth, is imprinted upon your parents' subconscious to give to you at birth. You can change your name later when you are on the Earth plane, but you will never lose the original name you came in with. It is the first registered name at birth. Occasionally the nurse at the hospital will misspell the name. If you never use the misspelled name or correct the error shortly thereafter, you would use the intended name, **not** the misspelled name.

If you really dislike your name—and many do—you can use

whatever name you like, the original name is never lost. This is important to remember. For the sake of understanding your plan, always work with your original full name. Do not use a confirmation name, a married name, a nickname, an adoption name or a changed name. If you have been adopted, you may want to look at both names—your birth name and your adopted name. It is interesting to note that the surname or last name is what we call in numerology an "Earth" name. You use this part of your name to help the family of origin with its group karma, which can go back many generations before it is balanced or corrected. For a woman to carry her husband's name, she actually assists him with his family's karma. That's an interesting thought to ponder. One thing I want to point out to you is that if you happened to be born with a name like "Baby Boy" or "Baby Girl Doe", usually this is immediately changed. In that case, you can use the changed name and NOT the "Baby Boy" or "Baby Girl Doe." It is also important to remember if there is a "Jr." after your name, you must include that in your name. But, you say, what if I was born with a Chinese name or Arabic name and letters? The same rule applies. The plan is based on vibrational, numerical forces in all languages.

I remember working with a gentleman who had used four different names by the time I did a reading for him. He had been in foster care, adopted, and been in prison. By the time I met him he was leading a very normal life working in an employment agency. I ignored his last three names and went back to his birth name. I also told him that he really should be working for himself, that this lifetime was intended for him to become independent, bold, entrepreneurial and a pioneer. Much of his frustration came from the fact that he had never done that. One day, five years later, he called and told me he had moved to Florida and had opened several travel agencies in different states and was hugely successful. He told me it was the reading that reflected back to him his own self. In the process, he gave himself the permission to quit his job and become his true person. The first birth name is the plan.

ஃ *Chapter 5* ೞ

Be True To Yourself

"What doth it profit a man, if he gains the whole world but loses his Soul?"—*The Bible*

A s previously stated, we know exactly what we are going to be working on and setting up while we are here in this particular life. If that is the case, then how could we be so blind to our own knowledge? What happens? Where do we get lost?

Several things happen. When we are little children, we seldom are given the tools to help ourselves uncover our path; certainly society doesn't encourage us as little children to be our own unique selves. We are more than likely put in a position where our parents and society will help us conform to what they think we should do or be. I recently did a consultation with a woman who was very unhappy working in the legal field. I asked her what she had wanted to do when she was younger. She told me she always wanted to be a nurse. I asked her why she hadn't. It seems her mother talked her out of it by telling her that all she would ever do is empty bedpans. Now she hates her job and feels she is too old to enter the profession she has longed for. It is never too late to experience some form of what you always wanted to do. Never, never, never give up on yourself and your heart's longing. You may not be able to be the brain surgeon you wanted to be, but you can still do some closely related endeavor. The person who wanted to be a famous singer can still sing in a church choir, with local groups, or entertain solo for shut-ins. You can still perform and express your gifts. Who knows what good things will happen to you when you are out there experiencing your heart's desire?

Eventually, the restrictions, upbringing, schools and other situations impose rules and regulations on us that stifle the intuition and knowledge that we started out with. We begin to rely on others and those outside ourselves for our directions and answers. We rely less and less on our own intuition and eventually erode trust in ourselves. When we lose trust in ourselves, we lose confidence as well. We don't have the confidence to follow our own path. Fear becomes a strong emotion. What if we do what we really want and fail or look foolish? What will people say? How will we survive? How will we pay the bills? We abandon ourselves.

When we lose our direction for our own lives, it can take many years before the pain of that loss is finally acknowledged. When a Soul reaches the Earth age of forties, it can become unbearable to be doing the wrong work in the wrong area. You never truly forget your own plan. It will always be there, vibrating and reminding you of a part of you that never came into being. It is my belief that one of the strongest reasons people are afraid to die is that they know there was "something" they were supposed to do and they did not or would not do it.

The more a person can be true to himself or herself in the direction of their lives, the more it benefits society as a whole. Imagine a society where we would be living our true paths and using our wonderful talents. Just think of how we all could benefit from that. Instead, we live lives of quiet desperation or "settling," believing that we can never be or do what is in our hearts. Remember, your Soul came here to learn, not to be comfortable. It did not come in to amass fortunes, run for office, live in poverty or work at the local convenience store. Through many experiences it will grow, but always keep in mind that it knows the direction it wants to go. These "jobs" are merely stepping-stones across the river to the other side of our destiny. We are not to get stuck on one of the stepping-stones. They are tools of instruction and grooming. When they have outlived their usefulness, we discard them and move on with other tools, always moving higher in awareness.

I hear often, from many of the people I have privately consulted with, that they are "too old," "have too many obligations or responsibilities," "have too big a house payment," are "too frightened," "their wives won't let them," "their husbands won't let them," and all the other reasons for not becoming their "true" self. I think the one I hear the most though, is "There's no money in it." A life is not about "There's no money in it." It is my belief after listening to so many people over the years, that they will enjoy their money more, be much happier, healthier and more at peace if they are doing what their destiny dictates. Remember what St. Thomas Logian said, *"If you bring forth that which is within you, what you bring forth will save you. If you do not bring forth that which is within you, what you do not bring forth will destroy you."* What you bring forth is your greater plan, the one you were intended to live and experience. It will never leave you while you walk upon this earth.

❧ *Chapter 6* ❦

Why Would You Reincarnate In The First Place?

"The Body of B. Franklin, Printer, Like the Cover of an Old Book, Its Contents Torn Out and Stripped of its Lettering and Gilding, Lies Here, Food for Worms, But the Work shall not be Lost, For it will as He Believed, Appear Once More, In a New and more Elegant Edition, Revised and Corrected By the Author."

Benjamin Franklin's epitaph, written by himself at the age of twenty-two.

Now you ask, why would we want to reincarnate in the first place? There are several reasons for this—a few of which I will mention.

1) **Balance karma**. What is karma? This term is tossed around society as a fairly scary word. You hear people say that he or she has good or bad karma. Karma is nothing more than a balancing act. If I punch you in the nose you can be sure somebody will punch me back. It may not be you, and it may take a few years or lifetimes, but I will be punched back. That's the balancing. You can see how one can accumulate karma after living many, many lives. We can

have batches of relatively simple karma and some that's extremely complicated. We wonder why certain good and wonderful people have such difficult and painful lives. You can be sure that there is some sort of karma being expressed in this particular life. There are no accidents on the Earth plane—even what appear to be accidents.

2) **Experience free will.** We are given the gift of free will by our Creator. Nobody can interfere with your free will. How can that possibly work? Wouldn't we all be running amok exerting our free will? We pretty much try to do that. When I speak of free will, I speak of the ability to choose how you will think about something. How you think will create decisions and actions based on your thinking. It is a learning lesson for all of us to learn how to use our will wisely. How to make wise decisions through the use of our free will. We are not all created physically equal, but we are equal in how we are given the use of our thinking. This has nothing to do with intelligence. If we knew how powerful the mind is, we would understand that what we think eventually gets out-pictured in our world. Through our time here on the Earth plane we are given the opportunity to use our free will wisely and to eventually combine our human will with our divine will to co-create our lives.

3) **Experience emotional energy.** We all know what that is. Just watch the greeting of a mother to one of her children whom she has not seen in a very long time, or watch the driver with road rage. Lots of emotional energy. When we are not on the Earth plane we can comprehend and intellectualize emotional energy but we cannot "feel" it. When we arrive on the Earth plane, we get to experience and "feel" all types of emotions, and through the use of our free will learn how to respond. It is through our responses and the result of our actions that we learn to grow and evolve. This is one reason why we will re-create the same situation in our lives over and over again until we have mastered the emotions and grown from them. Lots of

work for all of us in this area.

An important note to understand in this reincarnation process is that we do not reincarnate alone. What's that you say! Who came in with me? HELP came with you. When we are about to enter again into the Earth plane, we meet with our guides, who know our plan very well. It is during this process that we make an agreement with another Soul—normally someone whom we have known in prior lives—to accompany us on the journey. This Soul or Guide or Angel will be with us the entire time we are here on the Earth plane. They have agreed to stay with us until we take our last breath. They will help us, but only when asked. They cannot interfere with our free will. This is very important to remember—LEARN TO ASK FOR HELP.

Most of us do not ask for help. We try to do everything by ourselves. We were never intended to be here without a guide. These guides can give us energy when needed, open doors for us and assist in numerous ways. They cannot stop a karmic incident from happening, but can help you understand it and grow with it. They always reincarnate out of body. When you are ready to leave the Earth plane, they will go with you. The important thing to remember is that this guide is judged on how well he or she does with you for the Soul growth of the guide. Each of you learns. Now, if you are willing to take on more challenges, for instance go to medical school, try a new job, leave a marriage, do the work you love, etc, more guides will come in to assist you. These guides, however, are what I call "day guides". They work with you only on special projects. If you choose to stretch yourself and try on a new job etc. they will be there for the new job. If you do not choose to take the job, they do not come in to assist you. Many of our medical cures, famous music compositions and inventions were assisted from the other side by these guides working with individuals on the Earth planes. The point to remember is, you don't work alone. To really help yourself, learn to communicate through meditation, prayer or any way you choose with your guide. You are not alone. Ask with sincere intention.

Before you are ready to enter the Earth plane at the moment and time you have chosen, with your plan in hand, you must create your energy package. This is another important element of your life. When an energy package is being created, you will wait for the correct configuration of the heavens so that you are bathed in the harmony of the planets that are in alignment at the moment you take your first breath. It is at this time that you are magnetized at a cellular level by the planets' alignment. We call this astrology. You will have a specific Sun position for your ego, a Moon position for your emotions, a Mercury position for communications, a Venus position for your love nature, a Mars position for your drive and energy, a Jupiter position for your growth and expansion, a Saturn position for your discipline and structure, a Uranus position for your ability to make change quickly, a Neptune position for you to see into other worlds, and a Pluto position to help you transform and regenerate yourself. With your energy package and your name and date of birth, you are ready to enter into the dense, physical world and grow.

Use your energy package very wisely so that you do not burn up too much energy too early in your lifetime. This is one of the reasons we age. We do not know how to correctly use our energy. Most people become exhausted and burned out by the time they reach 50 years old, and literally start planning for old age and anticipate it from this period on. Just look at the greeting-card business to see what society thinks of individuals arriving at the age of 50. At the present time there are many Earth changes, and they will impact the length of time spent here on the planet. We will most likely be able to stay in our bodies longer, and perhaps complete our lessons. It is extremely important to maintain these bodies, as the sole purpose of your being here is to grow and evolve through your plan. It can be difficult to do this in an unhealthy body. Always, always remember, you did not come here to be happy, to be rich, to be poor, to be sad or whatever. You came here to grow, evolve and serve. Nothing else.

∾ *Chapter 7* ∞

The Most Important Birthdays—
the 7 Soul Cycle years

"Actions will be judged according to intentions"
—The Qur'an

When you are finished growing during this lifetime, you will discard the physical body that you were using during your stay and you will move on, taking with you only what you learned while you were here. Nothing more. People ask me all the time, what am I here to do? **YOU ARE HERE TO GROW**. It is as simple as that. You cannot take anything with you except what your Soul learned. Even your personality is dissolved. That is why it is very important to understand what it is you are to focus your time and energy on. When a person has no idea what they are to do here or what is their purpose, what happens eventually is that the person becomes what I call "divinely discontented." They don't like their jobs, they're in an unhappy relationship, they don't like where they live, and a whole series of "discontents" come into play. Sooner or later the Soul cries out for relief. We sometimes call these times "crisis" or dark nights of the Soul.

If you are wise, you will always pay attention to the voice whispering in your ear or your heart's longing beating in your chest. Listen carefully; it is trying to get your attention through your chatter, through your fears. Listen, because it is the small voice within that knows you well, it created you and it wants to experience its own plan. It will never go away.

So now you are here, ready to try again and learn more. Congratulations. You are now on your specific time frame. There is, however, another cycle of time always in effect that you must work with. It is called the "Soul Cycle." Remember, we said that the Soul has come in here to grow—not to be comfortable as so many think. The Soul retains all the information it learns while here on Earth. The personality does not. Remember, the personality you created to use here is not the Soul. You created a personality as a tool. You are not, however, a personality. When you have finished learning, you will dissolve the personality along with the body and move on, taking with you only what you learned.

The Soul will have the opportunity to collect and imprint this information every seven years. These are very important birthdays, and it begins the process at age 7. From age 7 to 8 is the first Soul Cycle year. The next one is at age 14, then 21, 28, 35, 42, 49, 56, 63, 70, 77, 84, 91, 98, 105, 112, and the last is 119 to 120—that is unless you remain longer. During each of these birthdays (lasting an entire year), the Soul imprints itself with what it learned during the previous six years—similar to a computer gathering and processing information. It is after you have finished each one of these ages that you grow tremendously in awareness. For instance, after you have reached age 29 or finished your 28th year of age, your growth in maturity blossoms. Now the individual can start her or his adult life. This is one reason why the divorce rate is so high between the ages of 28 and 32. The person wakes ups, realizes who he or she is and what he or she wants to do, and goes through tremendous change. It is actually after this age that you start your adult life. Prior to that time, you are finishing off karma with the family of origin.

After you have completed seven of these seven-year cycles, or the age of 49 to 50, you finally come into your own and start to be the most effective in your own life. You really don't know much about yourself until you have finished this seven times seven cycle. Now, if you knew that you continued to grow in awareness every seven years and that the most effective part was after the age of 50, wouldn't you look at your life on different terms? After the age of 50 you know more, you are aware of what you do and don't like, you have Soul-searched quite a bit and are free from the past "shoulds" of society, family and friends. Instead of preparing for old age, you now can be thinking very seriously about what it is you would really like to accomplish while you are here at this time on Earth. In fact, a good time to go to college is in your 70's.

It is actually very wise to see nature's cycles in the same seven-year pattern. It is my belief, that if we lived close to this seven-year cycle, we would be much healthier. There is a pattern in nature of the rule of seven. Seven days of the week, seven notes on a musical scale, seven colors in a spectrum, seven planets, the soil is to rest in the seventh year of planting, we are to rest on the seventh day, it takes seven years for ocean water to circumnavigate the globe and return to its original source. We are to rest our lives every seventh year—a sabbatical year, a year of recovery and rejuvenation and, of course, you have heard of the "seven-year itch." Where do you think that expression comes from?

During the first seven years of a Soul's life here on earth, the body is getting used to the environment. There is a big change after age 8, when the personality begins to go out more on its own. You see this in children where they begin to make up their own minds. Between 7 and 14 the mind or personality is being developed. From 14 to 21 years of age the emotions kick in, and from 21 to 28 there is an integration of the body, mind and emotions. It is only after this has all taken place and the transition away from childhood is completed—about 30 years of age—that the adult life begins. This is the reason you so often hear that expression "You can't trust anyone over 30." They have left their childhood innocence behind.

In addition to these seven-year cycles, each one has his or her own time frames built into the date of birth. We know when to start things, when to wait, when to let go, when to change, when to rest, when to harvest and when to plant. It's all in our date of birth. In our ignorance of this information we start things in an ending period so it can't work out, we stay stuck and won't make change in a changing period, we walk away from our harvest because we get bored, and a myriad of other actions when we are not in sync with our time frames.

Sometimes we have lived a charmed life for many years and all of a sudden the rug gets pulled out from underneath us. We have a reversal of fortune; our health goes bad, our spouse leaves, and a variety of life-altering experiences occur. We wonder what happened. How could we have seen it coming? So many times when we are given life's shocks it is for two reasons: 1) we have refused to grow through gentle means, so we are given a "cattle and stick" routine (death of loved one, reversal of fortune, health problems) to get us to take a deeper look at our lives and get back on the intended path. And 2) Karma was activated in our chart at a specific time—we, of course, are the ones who put that time frame in there to begin with. In either case, we are responsible for both situations. There are no accidents in the universe. If you always keep in mind that you are here for your Soul's growth—not to be comfortable, not to be entitled, not to live in a certain house, in a certain town with a certain job, then you will always check in with yourself to make sure you are growing in awareness.

I ask clients a certain question when they are wondering what they are here to do. I think it is very important to reflect on this question. If you received a call from the other side and they said, "Friend, we thought you were going to be here for another 40 years, but we have decided to bring you back sooner. In light of this then, please get your affairs in order, say goodbye to your family and friends, give away your treasures to those precious to you and be ready six weeks from today at 3 p.m. You don't have to worry about the details of how you will leave; we will take care of that. You will be healthy until the very last breath on Earth."

Okay, so now you receive this type of call and you are busy getting everything in order. About 2:55 p.m. six weeks from now, when you are ready to leave, you turn and look back and see your life and you say to yourself, I am so sorry I never did_____, or I could have started_____and somebody else could have continued on with it, or I always wanted to do_____but was too busy or afraid.

Whatever your answer is to this question, take a very hard look at it because it is your Soul's longing for what it never got to fulfill while here on the earth plane. Pay attention. You may never be given six weeks. Some people have a few years, others a few seconds. I believe it was Elisabeth Kubler-Ross who said, "We are all sitting on death row." It is a crucial question to ask yourself. Believe it or not, we are all in this position. We could be here another half hour or another 50 years. Our ego personality doesn't know. However, the Soul always knows; it always has. When it recognizes the correct time for it to depart, it will exit the physical body and move on. It doesn't matter whether you just got that raise or have ten kids to feed. It doesn't matter; you are "outta here." Keep this in mind as you live your life. Invest it very wisely. As the Buddhist tradition will tell you, live your life with wisdom and compassion, keep it balanced, grow in awareness and trust yourself. Remember the seven-year cycle.

Honor those birthdays. The Soul will take over the conscious mind and you will hear that voice telling you that you must make a change in your situation. Pay attention.

❧ *Chapter 8* ❧

Our Relationship with Numbers

"Numbers are the highest degree of knowledge. It is knowledge itself"—Plato

Figure (a)—draw the numbers as Ancients drew them.

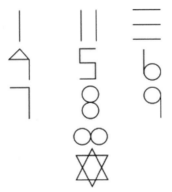

Numbers are not mathematics. They are symbols of specific qualities. They are specific vibrations. We can use numbers in mathematics, but they are not mathematics. They each have a specific essence—a force field, you might say. When you begin to understand the vibrations of numbers, you will be able to talk with people and "sense" that they have specific numbers just by how they speak and behave. The same can be said for "words."

Each word has specific numeric qualities. The word "love" is a 9 powered word—meaning the total of the numbers in this word add up to the single digit 9. The word "hate" is a 7-powered word. Every word you say is sending out coded signals or vibrational energies, forcing molecules to change shape.

When we say something enough times, or send out that energy enough times, it can come into manifestation. This again is why you hear these expressions: "Be careful what you wish for, you might just get it," or another expression taken from the Bible "By your words you will be praised or condemned." The rich get richer and the poor get poorer for several reasons. (One of the most powerful one is their speech). Rich people normally do not speak of lack and poverty. Poor people speak mainly of lack and poverty or of not having enough. Watch your words. Over and over again we unwittingly shoot ourselves in the foot by speaking ill will for ourselves. "I'm sick and tired," I'm dead tired," "I'm fed up to here" "You will break my heart," "My heart is broken," I could go on and on with all the energy we send out into the Universe creating damage to ourselves. It is not a laughing matter when we say things in jest. We need to be aware of our words and their power.

As you notice in Figure (a), the numbers are drawn to demonstrate their basic energies. As you look at these numbers you will notice that they have basically two shapes, the curve or circle and the straight line. These two shapes are the only shapes in nature. Others might say that the point or dot is the other shape. From this point comes the curve or straight line. It is interesting to see that in computer language, only the zero and one are used—the same shapes, the circle and straight line.

> Number 1)—Notice that this number stands by itself. It is independent and doesn't lean on anything else. It is an individual. It is an initiating spark. It is willful, courageous, pioneering and "I" centered. It is a masculine number. It

probes and modifies. It begins all things. Remember, we use the expression, "I want to be Number One." We usually don't say we want to be Number two. People who have a great deal of "1"energy have these characteristics. After a person has developed this willfulness, they move on to combine their will with somebody else's will. This is where the Number 2 comes in.

Number 2)—Notice that this number stands with another. It doesn't stand alone. It is as if two separate sparks must find a way to cooperate, compromise, keep the peace and be a team player in order to survive. It is an appreciation of another's will. It is receptive. Without this ability, the number 2 would not exist. It is patient, tactful, persuasive rather than forceful, and it is a feminine number. It is saying, I have mastered my independence and initiative but now I must learn how to use them with others in a way that is interdependent. This is where the cooperative nature of the "2" is imperative. After we have mastered the independence of the Number "1," the interdependence of the Number "2," we move out into the world through the Number 3.

Number 3)—Notice that this number combines the Numbers "1" and "2." It is as if the sperm (#1) meets the egg (#2) and combines them in a creative, expansive fashion. This is considered the creative number. It uses its creative expression in word, arts and design. We hear the Number "3" used a great deal in rituals. It is the result of the combination of two events or objects combining and creating something more than the total of the two. It just keeps creating. Many times an initiation is three days, 72 hours. "Jesus rose on the "3ʳᵈ" day." We also use three as a count to get things moving as is "1," "2," "3" go." We don't say "1", "2" go. We don't say two strikes and you're out at the old ball game. We say "three" strikes and you're out. After we have combined the numbers one and two to create number "3," the creative number, we must now ground this creativity into solid form, hence we arrive at the Number "4."

Number 4)—Notice that this number in Figure (a) contains a triangle on top of a #1. It is as if the #3, the creative result of the Nos. 1 and 2, is being grounded into the Earth. The Number "4" is the energy of the solid, earthy, structured, grounded, practical, and disciplined. These are all characteristics of this number. We think of somebody who is solid and a "straight-shooter" as being a "square." We don't call them a "round". This refers to the Number "4" energy. This number is disciplined, hard working, practical, and methodical. If we didn't have the energy of the Number "4" to solidify things and ground them, we would not see results for all the creativity that exists.

Number 5)—After we have had the results from the Number "4" and grounded the creative energy into form, it is time to make changes to it and make sure the energy doesn't get stuck. This is where the Number "5" comes into play. The Number "5" is a catalyst of change. It stands in the middle between Numbers 1 through 4 and Numbers 6 through 9. It looks backwards and forwards. Since it is in the middle and can see both sides, it knows how to make change more easily than any other number. In order to do this, it must have the freedom to do it. The Number "5" represents freedom, change, progress, flexibility, and the five senses.

Number 6)—This number always refers to love, domesticity, service, families, correcting social injustice, and a basic responsibility for the self and others. It is as if after the experience of the changes and freedom created by the Number "5," there is a settling in and concern for others and how all of this creativity is being cared for. If we look at this number, it almost looks pregnant. The Numbers "1" and "0" have combined—the individual and the creative source, the cosmic egg of the "0". The Number "6" also pertains to nourishment of the self and others. In fact, it is related to the food industry. There is a loving, healing and counseling quality to this number. Also, since it contains two Number "3's," it is very creative, perhaps even more than the Number "3" itself. This, therefore, is the number also of pregnancies, birth and marriage.

Number 7)—Notice the structure of this number. It almost tells you what it means—the self raised to a high level; the Number "1" crossed at the top. This number is the number of the higher self and represents mental power, spirituality, completeness, reflection, analysis, research, nature, the environment, rest, recovery and contemplation. It needs time for solitude to be able to figure things out. It is always trying to bring out the truth and a higher awareness. It is the passage of this Number "7" in our lives every seven years that creates an opportunity for us to recover, retreat, learn and complete a segment of our lives. Without this energy, we would not learn from our lessons. It encourages us to reflect and absorb all that we have learned. It encourages us to process this information so that we can move to a higher awareness of ourselves. It is basically a number that suggests discrimination and discernment.

Number 8)—Now, here is a powerful number for the material world. After humankind has mastered the other seven numbers, the Number "8" asks that the spiritual lessons of the previous seven numbers be integrated in the material world. The Number "8" is the number that combines the Spiritual with the material world. "As above, so below." This number has neither beginning nor an end. You can keep drawing it over and over without lifting the pen. When it is laid on its side, it represents the infinity sign. It can also be drawn as two triangles being combined, as shown in Figure (c). When these are brought together, they represent the Star of David. This number also, in the Hebrew context is considered the Number of God ("26"—a form of "8"). There is neither beginning nor an end to this number. The Number "8" stands for power and authority and continues to show up in areas where that is required. It always contains the lesson of learning to use power wisely and learning to use the material world wisely. If we are not able to combine the Spiritual into the material world, then the material world will continue to be harsh and a karmic campground. Once we are able to combine the two worlds, we ourselves become more Godlike.

Number 9)—Now that we have learned the meaning of all the other numbers, we must learn the finishing number, the number "9." The drawing of this number shows the Number "1" returning to the Divine Cosmic Egg, or the "0". This is the number of completion, letting go, for-giveness, detach-ment, service, giving without concern for what you get back. It is the final lesson. Because this number contains three Number "3's," it is also the number of beauty, art, charisma and love. The word "love" in fact is a nine-powered word. If I add all the letters up in this word, they will add up to a number "54." When I add the "5" and "4" together, it totals a "9." This number is all about becoming the humanitarian, the person who under-stands the human condition; the wisdom of all other num-bers is hidden within this number.

Now you know a little bit more about the vibration of each number. There could be volumes written on each one alone. For the sake of brevity, realize that our whole world vibrates using these energies. It doesn't matter what language you use, it is all numerically arranged. Each of us has different numeric codes that tell a tale of our lives on the Earth plane. _Some of the birth-name and birth-date plans we created for ourselves contain all the numeric vibration; others contains missing elements or numbers; still others contain an excessive amount of certain numbers. All this information is placed within your names and dates of birth. The discovery of your plan and your own time frames can be life saving and at the very least life enhancing_. The discovery of your own self and its' unique programming is available to you right now. Don't be lazy with your life.

Using the simple and easy steps of the next few chapters can put you on the true path for yourself. It can be compared to going around the block and meeting yourself again. Imagine being in a wilderness and finding a map that points to the way out and the rest stops and events that will be happening on the route. What a relief. You can have similar relief by understanding the map inside your name and birth date. You will know what to do in certain circumstances, why events happen, what types of jobs are best for you, what types of places you should avoid, the types of people and situation that nourish you and those that don't. You can understand the best time to begin something new, the best time to make change and the best time to let things go. Your name and date of birth is your treasure map to take with you wherever you go. You can never lose them.

❧ *Chapter 9* ❧

Your Major Life Path
or Learning Lesson

"God created the universe through the Breath of the Compassionate."—Mohammed

Let's talk first about your major Learning Lesson (also called your Life Path.) As previously mentioned, when you are about ready to enter the Earth plane you will choose a particular Learning Lesson or Life Path that will be your essence and your direction for your entire life. It is the path you walk, the style you live, the type of experiences that will come to you—in short it is your "way." You are here to learn the qualities of this number. It will color your life at all times and you will operate from its characteristics. It is your Soul's assignment to learn the lessons of this number. **You will, therefore, experience both the negative and positive qualities of this number.** This Life Path is found in your date of birth. If you are not sure of your date of birth (and believe it or not, some people do not know their date of birth), due to missing records or non-registration of your birth, always use the first recording of your date of birth. You cannot change your date of birth. You can forge some type of document later in life, but the original date of birth is your

entry point into this life. This is your map, your most important tool for your life.

By using your date of birth, you can discover what it is you have come in to experience and learn, and the time frame for the events in your life. Through very easy adding of the numbers of your date of birth, we discover your path. The formula is to add your month of birth to your date of birth to your full year of birth.

For example, if your date of birth were July 4, 1776 (the birth date of the United States), you would add 7 (July being the 7th month) to 4 (the day) to the total of the year 1+7+7+6 (the year adds up to 21). In other words, 7 + 4 + 21 = 32. Now we add 3+2 together and we get a 5. The Learning Lesson or Life Path of the United States or any one else who had that birthday would be "5."

July 4, 1776

  7
  4
  21   (1 + 7 + 7 + 6 = 21)
32 (3 + 2 = 5) Life Path #5

For another example, let's look at a celebrity—Madonna. Her birthday is August 16, 1958. Here again we add the month, August (8th month) to the day, (16) to the year 1+9+5+8 (23). We add the total of 8+16+23=47. Finally 4 + 7 = 11. Again we add the total 1+1=2. Madonna's Life Path is "11" Master Number or a final number of "2."

August 16, 1958

  8
  16
  23   (1 + 9 + 5 + 8)
47 (4 + 7 = 11) (1 + 1 = 2) 11/2 Life Path #11—2

When we look at numbers, always remember that there are only numbers 1 through 9. After these numbers, we begin the compound numbers or 10, 11, 12 etc. We still always are using just the numbers 1 through 9. If you totaled a compound number such as 11, 22, 33, 44, etc., you can reduce it to a single digit, but keep in mind, these are **Master Numbers,** and if you have reached any of these as your total, you are working on a special Life Path. There is much grooming to be done in association with your work, and hence your work may start later in life. Notice that Madonna has a Master Number 11/2 as her birth number, as does Bill Clinton. Before we start getting into the meaning of the Life Path numbers, I want you to really understand this simple addition before we move on. Please go back over this exercise. Remember, just ADD the MONTH to the DAY to the FULL YEAR. You will always reach a compound number. Add those together—even if one number is a zero—such as 40. (4+0= 4). Always notice if the compound number totals one of the double digits—a Master Number 11, 22, 33, or 44.

Now that you know your Life Path or Learning Lesson, let's look at what your Life Path number means for you.

Your Life Path or Learning Lesson

Number 1)
(If your number totaled 10, 19, 28, 37, 55, 64, 73, 82, 91 or 100)

In this lifetime you are learning the lesson of individuality, independence, self-reliance, self-assertion, self-development, leadership, innovation and the correct use of your will.

REVIEW: Those who have this Life Path function best in environments that foster self-reliance, courage, assert-iveness and decision-making. You are learning how to be in the forefront, take risks, but not be so willful that you run roughshod over others. Number 1's should be careful not to become too egotistical or arrogant. You are learning how to combine your human and Divine wills to co-create. You should pursue your own personal vision but at the same time respect other peoples wills. It's a delicate balancing act between extreme independence and cooperation. In a working environment, it is very important that individuals with this Life Path have a certain amount of independence to pursue their own unique ideas. You are excellent at creating ideas to get things moving again as well as modifying existing programs and companies.

Number 2)
(If your number totaled 11, 20, 29, 38, 47, 56, 65, 74, 83 or 92)

In this lifetime you are learning the lesson of patience, cooperation, partnership, sensitivity to the needs of others, the ability to follow as well as lead, diplomacy, the nurturing principle, being the peacekeeper, tact and persuasion instead of force.

REVIEW: Those who have this Life Path are learning to nurture others as well as themselves. This is a very sensitive number and it likes to be in partnership. Its general outlook is one of cooperation and sharing. You are very helpful in bringing the peace to difficult situations. You must guard against peace at any price (the doormat or the martyr). You are learning the art of compromise while maintaining your own personal dignity. To guard against excessive moodiness and sensitivity, you must harness your emotional responsiveness so that you can enhance the performance of the requirements you are here to accomplish. You make wonderful mediators and arbitrators. Since you can see both sides of an issue, you may enter the law profession. Number 2's must learn to be decisive and not just sit on the fence. There is a tendency to flip-flop or procrastinate. If this is a Master Number 11 behind the 2, you are very inspirational and very gifted in speech and in the arts. Your performance and words captivate the audience. Some of your performances may appear to be channeled from another world. Again, both Madonna and Bill Clinton have an 11 Master Number Life Path.

Number 3)

(If your number totaled 12, 21, 30, 39, 48, 57, 66, 75, 84, 93)

In this lifetime you are learning the lesson of how to use your creativity, self-expression and communication skills (writing, speaking). In addition, you are acquiring the qualities of sociability and charm. Above all, 3's must cultivate the use of words and bring joy to others' lives. You can make wonderful hosts, knowing always the right things to say. You must be careful, however, that you don't just say what others want to hear. 3's can make the mistake of superficial conversation and talk way too much. Overall you are attractive and can bring light and radiance to whatever environment you enter. You usually carry a positive attitude and a great deal of charm.

REVIEW: 3's should enter into occupations that provide them with an opportunity to use their self-expression. This can be in several areas, from fashion and art to decorating, music, writing and advertising. You are to express life through this creativity, beauty, friends and happiness. An important aspect of this expression is to stay very focused and hone your talent into a particular area. Although you may be creative in several areas, you must choose only one and really bring that gift up to its highest level. 3's must guard against sloppiness, over-talking, vanity, social over-achieving, jealousy, flirtatiousness, being scatter-brained, and the stretching or embellishing of the truth. Most people with this Life Path are in creative and expressive professions. Examples of 3 life paths are actresses Jodie Foster and Winona Ryder.

Number 4)

(If your number totaled 13, 22, 31, 40, 49, 58, 67, 76, 85, 94)

In this lifetime you are learning the lesson of how to apply yourself. While doing this, you will be learning the qualities of hard work, discipline, organizational skills, patience, endurance and a sense of order. Many builders and architects possess this Life Path (such as Donald Trump).

REVIEW: 4's are very hard workers and are learning to perform activities with a methodical, step-by-step approach. You are learning to avoid short cuts and get-rich-quick schemes. You are the builder and are practical, industrious, honest and the "salt of the earth" type of person. You are the person who gets hired to get the job done, similar to the power behind the throne. Using common sense, logic and effort, you build blocks of enduring life. The problem appears when you become too inflexible, too rigid in how things should be, too stubborn, and have a tendency to miss opportunities that might have made your project easier. It is important to remember, if you have this number as your Life Path, that you remain flexible and versatile and do not become the workaholic. It can make life miserable for you as well as for your family and co-workers—not to mention what it does to your health. As with all numbers, it is important to stay balanced. Remember to include play with your work.

A well-known No. 4 Life Path is Oprah Winfrey. She has learned to work hard, is very disciplined and produces her own show. From her hard work and creativity comes the tangible result. She will always be productive in her lifetime. The same goes for Elton John, another No. 4 Life Path. If your Life Path is Master Number 22/4 you will be learning to develop spiritual as well as practical qualities. Your Life Path will teach you to learn how to use your organizational ability to work with large-scale projects that bring about a greater good. It is possible to build a program or project that remains in place after your physical death. You are the visionary and can become the Master Builder of the New World Order.

Number 5)
(If your number totaled 14, 23, 32, 41, 50, 59, 68, 77, 86, 95)

In this lifetime you are learning the lesson of freedom and change. You must learn to adapt to many changes in your lifetime and use these changes as opportunities for your own development. This development will occur in the areas of your mental, physical, emotional and spiritual growth. Above all else, you are learning to understand and wisely use your freedom. There is a difference between constructive freedom and destructive freedom. In fact, the more disciplined you are, the more freedom you will have. You must have courage to seek the new and untried and let go of situations and people when they have outlived their usefulness. You must learn the law of discard without creating chaos in your life and in the lives of those around you. It is also important to understand how to transform the physical passions of the No. 5 into constructive activity. This is actually learning the law of energy transformation.

REVIEW: 5s' are freedom-loving, sexy (the five senses), curious, great teachers and healers and always the catalyst of change for others. Because your lives have so much change in them, there can be a great deal of restless energy. You must learn to eat very well to stay centered. Be careful you do not indulge in too much food, sex, drugs, alcohol, and rock "n" roll. All the environmental changes bring many places, persons and problems into your life. All of this provides abundant experiences from which you will, eventually, tame the lower nature in order to develop wisdom, character and Soul growth. 5's make great teachers, salespeople, trainers and promoters. You are able to speak any one's language—the rich, the poor, the young, the old, the brilliant and the average. Due to this ability, it is very hard to say "no" to a person with this Life Path. You can find another way to phrase your request so that you receive the answer you want. Any type of work that includes travel is a real plus, as you have a strong need to travel and be free.

A famous example of a 5 Life Path was Abraham Lincoln. He was a catalyst of change, bringing freedom and progress to the United States—which in turn has also a No.5 Life Path. The United States brings freedom and progress to the world.

Number 6)

(If your number totaled 15, 24, 33, 42, 51,60, 69, 78, 87, 96)

In this lifetime you are learning about responsibility, especially in the family area. You are learning about responsibility for the self and then for others. In doing this, there will be much service to others and many adjustments along the way. There is also a great deal of harmony with this number. Another form of harmony is music; so many times a 6 will have musical talent or enjoy singing. This is a nurturing number, and you may find those who have this Life Path to be involved in professions that do the same. A form of nurturing and nourishing others is in the food industry, or simply enjoying feeding others.

REVIEW: As a 6 you will have many adjustments to make in the home and community as you serve others. Sometimes there is a sacrifice of a certain aspect of the individuality in order to operate more effectively as part of a group. There can be many anxiety problems over others. As a 6 you may think you know what is best for others, or you may interfere in others' lives too often. This can make you too bossy, too self-righteous and a know-it-all. If you go to the other extreme, you can become a doormat. You have a need to be needed and may bring needy people into your life so you can rescue them and be needed. 6's make wonderful healers, teachers and counselors. If you run a business, you may have responsibility for many employees and their families.

President George W. Bush has a 6 Life Path. His is a Master Number 33/6 and, therefore, has an element of sacrifice of his own needs to serve the community. Master Number 33 always has a lesson to learn regarding how to relieve the suffering of humankind. 33's must first see their own self-righteousness before they can successfully serve.

Number 7)
(If your number totaled 16, 25, 34, 43, 52, 61, 70, 79, 88, 97)

In this lifetime you are learning to perfect your mind and expertise. This can take many paths, but it will always lead you to the development of your mind and knowledge. 7's are also working on the development of the higher self. This is why during the 70's of the last century there were so many "self-help" movements in America. Seven's need their privacy and space, and the rich inner world of the mind is very important to them. You also need to be around smart people—people who spark your mind. You do not tolerate stupid behavior very long. Education should be emphasized. Advanced degrees, certificates, credentials should be sought. Indeed, there is a need to specialize. The 7 is a highly spiritual number, and in the ancient days, if you had this number you would have been removed from your family to be raised by temple priests.

REVIEW: 7's need to figure things out for themselves rather than from friends' advice. There is a need for time alone and to make up your own mind. Due to your smart, analytical mind, you can sometimes be sarcastic, critical and judgmental. You don't tolerate fools very well, and will tell the truth even if it is unpopular. You have a sound mind and are often sought after for your ethics and analysis. You want to know how things work. There is always an element of learning FAITH over FEAR on this Life Path. Because of this, 7's may have many tests of their faith until it is solidified. They need time in nature. It helps you to balance your heart with your intellect. If you become too intellectual, you can be very lonely and cut off from your heart energy. 7's make great teachers and will usually arrive in a teaching situation. This can take the form of a college professor or teaching ancient healing techniques to a small group of New Age students.

John F. Kennedy Jr. had this Life Path, as does the comedian/producer Mel Brooks. Now there are two unique examples of the same number.

Number 8)
(If your number totaled 17, 26, 35, 44, 53, 62, 71, 80, 89, 98)

In this lifetime you are learning how to use your power and authority wisely, as well as how to combine the spiritual in the material world. You are a born leader and must learn all the nuances of learning to use your resources for the highest and best good. What are these resources? They are time, energy and money. You will be instructed in this lifetime how, where and with whom to invest these resources. Eight is considered the number of God in the Hebrew alphabet. By learning the lesson of this number, the combining of spiritual principles in the material world, you can become more Godlike. As with any number, there can be extremes. We see many of those with this Life Path using power to the extreme.

A prime example of this is Joseph Stalin who had the Life Path of 8 and Edgar Cayce, the famous mystic who had a Master Number 44/8 Life Path. Power can be benevolent or destructive.

Over time we have seen many leaders with an eight Life Path—Stalin, Boris Yeltsin, former senator Bob Dole, Chicago's Cardinal Bernardin and Edgar Cayce.

REVIEW: Since this Life Path is always instructing in the correct use and not abuse of power, it is important to be involved with powerful people. Attend power breakfasts, lunches, etc. Get used to using your power. You are the visionary and the leader and must practice leading. You are not a follower, nor will you be comfortable in a secondary role. You should learn about money, how it works and the value of it. It is important to avoid greed, manipulation, controlling, exploiting, and the negative qualities of abusive power. This is a number that also controls the sports world. It is not unusual to see those well known in the sports world and who have this Life Path to eventually enter the business world. 8's are usually born into a family where there are power struggles as an instruction to learn how to use power. If your Life Path is a 44/8, this is an indication that in past lives you gained a great deal of power but sometimes through ruthless means. This lifetime is an opportunity to balance out this Karma by putting your energies to work for the world's underprivileged. Your goals should be directed towards benefiting large numbers of people. Always come from the highest intention when leading.

Number 9)
(If your number totaled 18, 27, 36, 45, 54, 63, 72, 81, 90, 99)

If this lifetime you are learning to be the universal helper. This is a lesson in compassion, forgiveness, generosity, service and fine arts. The nine is a finishing number. After you have learned all the lessons of the prior eight numbers, you can now learn to let go, detach and serve. This is the highest number of beauty. It contains three 3's, and we ultimately say a person is "dressed to the nine's." Many times those who have this number are involved in the art world or a benefactor to the art world. 9's also possess a great deal of charisma. Since it is a finishing number, you are learning to be in this world but not of this world, to use this world but not to depend upon this world. This does not mean this is the last incarnation for you. It means that you have chosen to learn the qualities of this vibration.

REVIEW: 9's must learn to let go and not cling to things of this world. Imagine a person entering a room with a big sack on his or her back. This sack contains knowledge and wisdom from that person's prior lives. This is a picture of someone with a 9 Life Path. You are filled with wisdom and knowledge and are seen by others as a sage. Because of this, you make an excellent psychologist or teacher. You see others in their full potential and have the ability to help them towards that vision. You must be careful not to be used by friends, family and strangers. Because you have such wisdom and good ideas, others may use you for this purpose and then later drop you. It is essential that you not worry about where your good is coming from. You are well protected by the higher forces if you are living up to your numbers and serving humanity.

A prime example of a 9 Life Path is Mahatma Gandhi. He devoted his life to service. If you cling to things of this world, the things you cling to can be removed by fate. This can be a house you must have, dependency on a certain source of income, dependency on a spouse, etc. You must cling to the eternal or life can be very difficult for you. "Let go and let God" is the motto for this number. Give without worrying what you get back. You will receive it back, but not necessarily from the recipient of your gift. You do very well with charitable groups, as well as the art and theater world. You are a wonderful teacher. If you have a 9 Life Path, remember that you will feel alone even in a crowd of friends. You are always somewhat detached so that you can serve more effectively.

℘ *Chapter 10* ℘

Your Motivation (Soul Urge), Personality and Destiny

"Use the light that is in you to recover your natural clearness of sight."—Lao-tzu

Figure (b) **THE NUMBERS IN YOUR NAME**

ACH LETTER HAS A NUMBER. For example, the letter "A" is a 1, "B" is a 2. All the letters of the alphabet are listed here. Their numbers are placed next to them:

A	=	1	J	=	1	S	=	1
B	=	2	K	=	2	T	=	2
C	=	3	L	=	3	U	=	3
D	=	4	M	=	4	V	=	4
E	=	5	N	=	5	W	=	5
F	=	6	O	=	6	X	=	6
G	=	7	P	=	7	Y	=	7
H	=	8	Q	=	8	Z	=	8
I	=	9	R	=	9			

Now, in the space below, please print (in large letters) your entire name as it is on your Birth Certificate. Include your middle name. Do not include a baptismal name, married name, nickname or adoption name unless the original name was replaced very shortly after birth. Under each letter place a number, using the list above. If you had a misspelling on your birth certificate but never used the misspelled name, use the correct name as it was supposed to be.

Now total all the numbers of your name. What number did you get? Pay attention to double digits such as 11 or 22.

Add the total together. Example: A total of 71 would be 7+1=8. The final total would be 8. This final number is called your DESTINY NUMBER. This is what you are trying to accomplish. It has to work in conjunction with your Learning Lesson/Life Path. This is your Destiny, the direction for your life.

Your full name at birth.

What numbers are missing in your name?
List them here _____

What is in a name? Everything! You are about to take a look at your Soul Urge and Motivator, your Personality, your Destiny (what you are striving to become) and your Karma. Take your time. Now that you have figured out your Learning Lesson number, let's look at your name at birth. I repeat, use only the first registered name at birth, with the exception as noted earlier.

(Do not use your married name, baptismal name, adopted name or nickname. Do use Jr. for junior.)

Each letter has a specific number assigned to it. For example the letter "A" is 1, "B" is 2, "C" is 3 etc. Notice in Figure (b.) there are three rows of letters, A through I, J through R, and S through Z. By using the letters of your full name (including middle name) and the numbers assigned to each letter in Figure (b) assign a number to each letter of your full name. I have simplified the numbering of the letters. For instance, the letter "V" is the 22nd letter of the alphabet. Instead of using the number 22, we simplify the number to (2+2=4) and use "4" instead.

Notice the example of the name Abraham Lincoln, who was born February 12, 1809. He has a Life Path of the Number 5.

2 (the 2nd month of February) + 12 (the day) +1+8+0+9 (the year totals 18)

His Life Path is computed by adding 2 + 12 + 18 for a total of 32. We add the 3+2 together for a total of 5 or a "5" Life Path. He is a 32/5.

His name, ABRAHAM LINCOLN, tells us the power and direction of his life. It also tells us about his karma, which we will talk about in a later chapter.

Vowels in his name are A,A,A,I,O, for a total of "9." We understand quite a bit more about President Lincoln and what was deep inside motivating him. His consonants total 42. Adding the 4 & 2 together. We see that his consonants total 6. This was what we saw—his outer personality. When we total these together—9 vowels and 6 consonants, we total 15. When we add 1 and 5 together, we total 6. The number 6 was what he was striving to become (otherwise known as his Destiny).

To understand your own numerical vibrations, you can do the

same simple exercise.

Add up the numbers in the vowels—just the vowels. <u>ALWAYS COUNT "Y" AS A VOWEL unless it is the first letter of the name.</u> (If the first letter is a Y and sound like an "E" or a vowel sound as in "Yvonne", you can use it as a vowel as well.) Add up the numbers in the consonants—just the consonants. You will have two different totals, the **vowel total** and the **consonant total.** Now, remember the two different totals but **add these two totals together** for a third total. Again see the name of Abraham Lincoln for an example. Did you get a Master Number in your totals?

What you have just discovered by adding up the <u>vowels</u> is the *Soul Urge or Motivator* in your life: where you are coming from, what drives you, what people may not know about you. It is always related to recent past life experience. Some numerology books call this the "Soul Urge" or the "Heart's Desire."

What you have just discovered by adding up the <u>consonants</u> is the *Personality* you created for yourself, how people will see you, the type of behavior you will use as a tool here on the Earth plane.

What you have just discovered by adding the <u>two totals together</u> is your *Destiny,* or what you said you would try to accomplish before leaving the Earth plane. These numbers are your codes, and it is your assignment to learn how to work with all of them.

Let's begin with the total of your **vowels** We will now put meaning to the letters a, e, i, o, u and "y." The vowels always reveal the deeper part of a person. What you may *see* is the personality and the actions taken by an individual. What you may *not see* is what is driving them to think, be and act a certain way. We always come from our "Vowels," our "Soul Urge," and our "Hidden Motivator." *It is what you have done in recent past lives.* What is comfortable for you? What you know. For those who are beginning to learn about the vibrations of numbers, this is the energy you sense about a person. Many times a person will hide this part of himself or herself very well. When someone realizes that a person is coming from a totally different place than they had thought, it can cause problems in the relationship. They find out about a part of a person they didn't know existed. It provides a picture of the "real" person. Remember, all numbers work in conjunction with other numbers in your name and date of birth.

Your Soul Number— the total of your vowels

If your vowels total up to the Number 1:

You are really very independent deep down. You don't want somebody to tell you what to do. You like to be in charge and have the ability to create innovative ways to solve problems. There have been many lives where you had to do things on your own without support from others. In this lifetime, you may have challenges learning how to work well with others, particularly in partnerships.

If your vowels total up to the Number 2:

You really want and need to have a partner to be happy. Deep down, no matter how independent you may seem to others, you really want to do things with a partner. You also could be a bit indecisive due to the fact that you see both sides of everything. There is a tendency to procrastinate. Deep down you are always seeking peace and dislike confrontation, and probably are more sensitive than others realize. You may need to be more decisive and independent. It depends on what other numbers are in your name and date of birth.

If your Vowels total up to the Number 3:

Deep within you are always coming from a creative and pleasant point of view. No matter how business-minded or scientific minded you may appear, from within you want and need to be creative. This is particularly true of using the written and spoken word in your creativity. It is essential that you find creative outlets for yourself. This number gives you the ability to be very charming, perhaps too talkative, and fun. You know how to use words effectively.

If your Vowels total up to the Number 4:

You are coming from a place of order and structure. You like to work hard and want to be productive. You can be a bit rigid (depending, of course, on what other numbers influence you) and need to make sure that you stay in balance regarding your work. You are usually tireless in your work and are not happy if you don't see results for your labor. Learn to be more flexible. There is a very conservative side with this number, and you may surprise your friends by exhibiting this side of you.

If your Vowels total up to the Number 5:

You are coming from a strong need for freedom. You have in recent past lives been very free and were used to change. In this life you don't want to be bored, and no matter how hard you work or how organized your life, you will always choose freedom as your basic need. Of course, that can go to the extreme. You could possibly act out the need for freedom too much by leaving jobs prematurely, have problems committing in relationships, and indulging in various ways. Working with this need is the challenge.

If your Vowels total up to the Number 6:

You are coming from a place of responsibility and caring. Deep down you need to be needed, so you may create situations in your life where you will be needed. Also, you will find yourself in roles where you will counsel and teach people. At times you may think you know what is best for others and may interfere too much. At other times you may let yourself be used too much. You are very committed to family and home, and nurture others through food. You might love to cook. It is another form of nourishing others.

If your Vowels total up to the Number 7:

You are coming from a place of introspection and have spent lifetimes developing your higher mind. You need to be around smart people, people who spark your mind. You need to be alone more than most people realize. Because of this, others may misunderstand you. You like to reflect, analyze and figure things out by yourself. It is not easy for people to deceive you, as you have developed discernment from your past lives. You come from the truth. There is a strong need to be in the world of nature.

If your Vowels total up to the Number 8:

You are coming from a point of power. You have been a very powerful person in past lives, and understand how power and authority works. You are very ambitious and can be driven deep within to have power again. You see the big picture and like to think big. It is difficult to not be in a position of power yourself. You don't like to think small. For those who do not realize this aspect of you, they will be very surprised when you demonstrate it. You understand how the material world works and can help others to become powerful themselves.

If your Vowels total up to the Number 9:

You are coming from a point of service and assistance. You have been a humanitarian in past lives and you understand the human nature very well. You understand how people suffer. In this lifetime you will be driven deep within to help people and will not be happy unless your work is benefiting others. Even if you are the head of a big corporation, deep down inside you will want your money and/or your company to help others. You make a natural psychologist for others. There is always the element of aloneness in your life. This is really detachment you have learned from other lives. There is a soft touch within you that resonates to others' sufferings. You also have a strong appreciation for art and beauty.

If your Vowels total up to the Number 11:

See the information for the Vowels totaling up to Number 2. Vowels totaling 11 signify past life experience as a Light Worker. You are bringing into this life the qualities of peace and inspiration. You know how to shine your light so others may see. Deep within you are very connected to the other side and can channel information.

If your Vowels total up to the Number 22:

See the information for the Vowels totaling up to Number 4. In addition to the need to be productive, you have in past lives been capable of building programs and structures that have had a lasting impact on humanity. You come from a place of vision and can improve the lives of many through practicality and beauty.

If your Vowels total up to the Number 33:

See the information for the Vowels totaling up to the Number 6. You have been a "Cosmic Father/Mother" in past lives. People brought their troubles to you and you helped them. You come from a place of broadmindedness, beauty, love and kindness. You are like a refuge for others. You are capable of seeing the Divine when others cannot.

If your Vowels total up to the Number 44:

See the information for the Vowels totaling up to the Number 8. You have been a "Spiritual Warrior" in past lives. Your heart's desire is to make spiritual issues practical to improve the world. You contain logic, common sense and great resourcefulness. This can help in overcoming everyday problems. There is a sincerity and directness in your nature. You hate to be kept waiting, and dislike things left undone or poorly finished. You attract power, and people feel secure in how you will treat them.

Your Personality—
the total of your consonants

Now take a look at the total of your <u>consonants.</u> The numbers behind these letters should have totaled to a double-digit number. Remember to add these together to get a total single digit. We always like to see the double digit, though, to determine if it is a Master Number. Master Numbers are 11, 22, 33 and 44. The consonants show others what type of personality you are using in this lifetime. This is how people see you. It is important to remember that you are not your personality. It is simply a tool you have created for this particular life. Remember, when you are ready to leave this lifetime you will dissolve the personality and the physical body. The personality serves you; you do not serve it. The ego is very connected to the personality. Many times we get caught up in our personalities forgetting who we really are. Over time and perhaps with a few harsh lessons, we learn to master our own personality. We learn to know when it doesn't serve us very well and we make the necessary changes to it. Remember, it serves us, not vice versa.

Learning to master the personality can take many, many years. When you hear someone say they are never going to change, do not believe them. Their core center of what they brought forward from past lives doesn't change, but their personalities can change a great deal. I have seen very stubborn and stuck individuals wait until they have experienced 10 of the seven-year cycles (or the age of 70) before they begin the change. You cannot change anyone; the person must want to change him or herself. It doesn't work any other way. Remember what I said earlier—we are all on our own timetables. No Soul is ranked. Each seventh birthday gives us the opportunity to grow in awareness.

I am frequently asked the question "What am I here to do?"

The answer is simply to grow. Just grow. It is important to remember nobody is entitled here. Is a Soul who labors 18 hours a day in Bangladesh for very little remuneration less entitled than a Soul who labors eight hours a day in Boston? We are not here to be rich, poor, sad or happy. We are here to grow and learn. All of our knowledge learned from the Earth experiences goes with us when we leave. So now take another look at your own personality. Detach from it a bit and understand that you are not your personality. You only created this personality for this particular life. During another life, you might create a very different personality. If you are very shy in this lifetime, you might decide in a future life to reincarnate with a wild and crazy personality. It all depends on what will work best for you so that you can easily grow.

If your consonants total Number 1
(10, 19, 28, 37, 46, 55, 64, 73, etc.):

You will exhibit a very independent and willful personality. You like to initiate things on your own. You need a very strong, patient and supportive personality for your life to work well, even though you think you can do everything yourself. There is a need to be first, and possibly you could be self-centered. You like to be the leader, and might find it difficult to accept orders from others. You are definitely not a follower type of personality. You work best in situations where you can be independent and original. Many people who are entrepreneurs have this personality number. In a love relationship, you can be very direct and dislike small talk. If this is your personality number, learn to master a strong ego and be watchful that you don't try to exploit others for your own gain. So much depends on other numbers in a chart. You may have enough 2 energy. If so, that will soften the willfulness of the 1 personality.

If your consonants total Number 2
(11, 20, 29, 38, 47, 56, 74, etc.):

You will exhibit a very sensitive and vulnerable personality. A 2 personality can be somewhat indecisive and very uncomfortable in a situation where they have to choose. This personality is experienced as the peacekeeper—the person who wants to be diplomatic, persuasive and tactful. You dislike the use of force to get what you need and will avoid doing it. Many times someone who has created this personality for this lifetime may have had a very brusque, bossy personality in prior lives. They want to balance that personality with a softer one. 2 personalities make excellent negotiators and arbitrators, so the law profession is excellent for you. You drive yourselves crazy with indecision and procrastination. You can sit on the fence for many years, paralyzed for fear of making the wrong decision. I always tell clients who have a predominant 2 in their chart, particularly if it is their personality, that the "Universe loves a made-up mind." It is important to be decisive and to not stay stuck in indecision.

If your 2 is comprised of an 11 or those numbers totaling an 11, you have a Master Number for your personality. There is a luminous quality about you. People will be drawn to you for your light. You are even more sensitive than the average 2. This is always the number of the Light Worker and Channeler—someone who is very connected to the unseen world. Make sure you associate with highly evolved people. Do not waste your time with those who are not. You are the visionary. The word "Light" totals to 11.

If your consonants total Number 3
(12, 21, 30, 39, 48, 57, 66, 75, etc.):

You will exhibit a very pleasant manner. You think of yourself as charming, somewhat talkative and a great host or hostess. There might be a tendency to exaggerate or embellish the words just so they sound better. That can be used to describe a negative experience as well as a positive one. You can say a great deal without really saying anything of substance. It is important not to be superficial in your words; not to just say what you think someone else wants to hear rather than what you truly think or feel. If you are not sincere in your speech, you may find yourself talking too much as a form of releasing nervous energy.

Another quality of this personality is the joy you have the opportunity to deliver. Not only can you spread joy, but you can also spread optimism. It is the number of the perpetual romantic. Many people in the acting and creative fields have this personality. They are usually very attractive people and have a certain flair in clothing. Above all else, the 3 must learn not to scatter its creative talents. You can sing, write, act and design. It is important to focus one of these so that the talent can be fully developed.

If your consonants total Number 4
(13, 22, 31, 40, 49, 58, 67, 76, etc.):

You will exhibit a very hard-working, productive, detailed and disciplined personality. You might have a Number 5 Soul, a hidden motivator, but you will appear to be just the opposite. You are the person most people would love to hire, because you would get the job done. Unfortunately, you can get stuck in the trees and forget there is a whole forest out there. This is the number of the proverbial workaholic. You can get carried away with work and order and all the details. You can make it very hard for those around you, as you expect that most people should work as hard as you do. Because you can get stuck in the details with a somewhat limited viewpoint, you can miss opportunities that might come along to make your life easier.

You are very practical and prefer security to taking risks, even though your life might be easier if you took them. There is a strong loyalty in this personality and you really pride yourself in your work. If you are not careful you can box yourself in. Remember the number 4 is represented by a square. If you become too stuck or too stubborn in your thinking, you can develop the diseases of rigidity—arthritis and hardening of the arteries. There is a need for play and fun with this personality. You really like routine and hate to waste time.

If you have a Master Number 22/4 personality, you should attract into your life situations that will improve the standards for the human race. You can use your hard work and discipline to better the standards in a very tangible way. For example, you could become involved in a program that creates buildings for the homeless, or create a program that provides practical relief for the working poor. As with all Master Numbers, you need to associate with very evolved people. You will not be satisfied with relationships that are not Spiritually bonded. Many Nobel Prize winners have a prominent 22 in their name or date of birth.

If your consonants total Number 5
(14, 23, 32, 41, 50, 59, 68, 77, etc.):

You have a personality that loves freedom and change. You hate to be bored, and others may see you as somewhat restless. You love adventure and activity, and may leave a situation too early due to the fact that you thrive on change. You can be very difficult to tie down, always seeking the back door of escape. Consequently, you could be challenging in close personal relationships, as you might see them as a threat to your need for personal freedom. Of course, much depends on other numbers in your chart that balance out this strong freedom-loving personality.

A 5 personality has a way of speaking anybody's language. That means you can change like a chameleon to adapt to the situation in which you find yourself. You can be witty and sexy and a bit indulgent in the five senses. You must be careful that you don't become too involved in too much food, sex, gambling and joie de vivre. To be tied down to a boring desk job is not your cup of tea. You will find many excuses to leave the office. It would be better to create a career where you have much freedom of movement. You can draw from many of your unusual experiences to relate stories and lessons that help teach people how to make constructive change in their lives. If your personality becomes too indulgent in sensual delights, the area of the body that is affected is the digestive tract. Anyone with a 5 Personality or a 5 Life Path takes in much more of life than any other number. They are, therefore, more prone to digestive and elimination problems. They just cannot digest all that it wants to take in.

If your Consonants total to the Number 6
(15, 24, 33, 42, 51, 60, 78, etc.):

You exude the quality of the responsible one. Others see you as the person who would make sure everybody is taken care of. You have the personality of the Cosmic Mother/Father. Here is the personality that needs to be needed. You will, therefore, find yourself in situations where you will be called upon to rescue, comfort and give advice. You can think you know what is best for others, so you could be a bit bossy and self-righteous. This can also leave you wide open to being used. If people don't appreciate all your help and assistance, you can be indignant and manipulative. Because of your strong need to be needed, you may at times manipulate others so they will continue to need you.

Above all else, this personality number is filled with love and harmony. In fact, those who created this personality for themselves may be musically inclined. There is also a touch of the artist here. A very interesting quality of this personality is the strong need to correct social injustices in our society. Those who have the number 6 as their personality number may find themselves in social activism. They want to see that the wrongs in society are corrected. It is not surprising to see your personality often employed in social-welfare endeavors, healing arts, counseling and teaching. A 6 personality worries quite a bit, so they too, like the number 5, suffer from digestive problems. A caution for this number is to stay away from sweets and creamy foods. You love them too much for your own good health. Those who have a 33/6 personality have an element of sacrifice in their personalities. They will give up some of their own wishes to help and serve. This is very much a Mother Teresa type of personality.

If your consonants total to the Number 7
(16, 25, 34, 43, 52, 61, 70, etc.):

You are seen by others as a bright-minded person. You appear quite smart, very analytical, curious and somewhat private. You need the space to be alone and away from the roaring crowd. You like to figure things out for yourself. You don't want others to give you their answers. You like research and like to dig deeply to uncover solutions. This is a somewhat refined personality and definitely the deep thinker. You have what others would call a sound mind. You don't take things at face value, as you question people's motives. It is not easy for someone to fool you. You can "read" them very well. There is a refinement about you. Others might call it aloofness.

Due to the fact that the 7 personality stays in its mind for the most part, there is a challenge to combine the heart with the head. If this cannot be done, the 7 Personality can find itself quite lonely. "To analyze love is to lose it," the old saying goes, and this couldn't be more appropriate than for a 7 personality. If you have created this personality number for yourself, it is important that you not analyze everything. The potential to be critical and judgmental is very strong with your personality. This could alienate the very people you want to attract. In your love relationships you need someone who is mentally compatible, as you love bright people, people who spark your mind. Walks in nature, meditation and reflection are all nourishment for your personality.

If your Consonants total to the Number 8
(17, 26, 35, 44, 53, 62, 71, 80, etc.):

You appear to others as a leader. You do not like secondary roles. Your personality is very strong, and you want to be in charge. You see the big picture. It is comfortable for you to be around people in power. You don't like to do all the details of a project, and would rather hire others for those roles. There is a strong competitive nature about you. This can be quite challenging in a partnership, especially in marriage. You like the good life, a nice home, car and the rest of the trappings. If you do not have power, you can behave almost in a tyrannical way. This can be very difficult in the partnership. You must try to really understand how to work with the material world. There is a tendency to give money too much value. You must be careful to understand the true value of money, what it is and what it is not.

Since the number 8 in the Hebrew alphabet is the Number of God (26), you have a personality in this lifetime that can combine the Spiritual with the material world. In fact, when you are truly practicing this combination, you appear more Godlike. When you combine the Spiritual with the material world, you are never afraid of anyone becoming more powerful than you. If anything, you devote yourself to helping others experience their own power. This is especially true if you have the 44/8 combination. If you are a 44/8, you can be the visionary who sees a new type of world order—new cities, new governments and new ways of doing business. You can help us create our programs in line with your visions.

If your consonants total to the Number 9

(18, 27, 36, 45, 54, 63, 72, 81, 90, etc.):

You appear to others as the sage filled with wisdom. You appear to be the humanitarian, the universal helper. In this lifetime you wanted to be able to express service through your personality. You will, therefore, be seen by others to be the psychologist. People will cry on your shoulder and bring you their problems. You must learn to say "no," or others will continue to use you. An added bonus with this number is that you will always appear to be younger than your age; people usually are not able to guess your age. Others may be very jealous of you; be prepared for this. They are jealous of your ability to be prophetic and wise. Others may be very drawn to you. They want your wisdom and assistance. Your personality must learn to let go; this is imperative.

You also have a great eye for beauty, art and poetry. This is where the expression "dressed to the nines" comes from. You are the epitome of beauty, the height of loveliness. There is a charisma about you (hence the jealousy). You are the dreamer and the idealist who longs to make this world better. You must hold fast to your dreams, as we need this personality to help us be aware of your vision. The 9 personality has an international quality to it. There should be remarkable people and adventure in your life. The world belongs to you with this number. The question is how can you wisely serve the world through this personality you created for yourself.

Your Destiny
(what you said you would strive to accomplish, the total of all letters)

Now you have a better picture of the Personality you are using in this lifetime, as well as what motivates and drives you. Just understanding both of these can be a great help in realizing why you behave and think a particular way. When we add these two together, we arrive at our **Destiny** The Destiny is always found by **adding up the total letter count in your full birth name**. This is what you said you would like to accomplish before you leave. This is what you are striving to become. Many people think quite narrowly in what they would like to accomplish. For example, a person who wants to become a physician might pigeonhole himself or herself into the area of pediatrics. The Destiny might say, though, that the Soul wants to really accomplish becoming a healer—a broader prospective. You can accomplish being a healer by being a pediatrician, a massage therapist or a nutritionist; all of them are healers. You get to pick which one you would like to focus on and accomplish. That is your free-will choice. To say that you can only be a pediatrician would be self-limiting. What if you couldn't be a pediatrician through family circumstances or other factors? Could you not still be a healer?

If your full name totals to the Number 1
(37, 46, 55, 64, 73, 82, 91, 100):

You are striving to become in this lifetime a very independent person. It doesn't matter if your chart is filled with several 2's. You want to become more risk-taking, more entrepreneurial, more courageous, more willful, more innovative, more independent and more inventive. You are trying to use your will wisely and want to learn to combine your human will with your Divine will so that you can co-create. It is important not to run roughshod over others but to instead notice the effect your willfulness has on others and their reac-tion to you. You want to know what it is like to be sort of the "Lewis and Clark" pioneer who takes risks and doesn't live life looking back over your shoulder won-dering what other people will say or think. You want to become a person who is not afraid to initiate a new program, a new product, and a new idea. You want to accomplish in this lifetime the development of your will. This can take many forms. You can have your own busi-ness, run for political office, invent a new product or service, be an avant-garde artist or explore the great unknown of space. The development of this aspect of you can take many forms. Again, you get to choose. Just remember the bigger reason.

If your full name totals to the Number 2

(29, 38, 47, 56, 65, 74, 83, 92,101):

You want to become a peaceful, cooperative and dip-lomatic person in this lifetime. You want to understand partnerships and how they work. You are willing to com-bine your own will with that of others so that you can work in a cooperative spirit. You are cultivating patience in this lifetime. You are striving to become the peacekeeper who sees both sides of all issues, to assist in bringing peace to warring factions. You want to practice interdependence rather than independence. You are trying to become the example of kindness and tact, using persuasion rather than force to accomplish the best solution for the highest and best good of all parties. At the same time, you are striving to make decisions without procrastination. You want to learn to pay attention to de-tails without getting stuck in them. Because you know how much gossip can hurt others, you are striving to avoid using it. There are interests in the law and mediation where you can use your gifts. Your acute sensitivity makes you aware of others' needs and feelings, and you can help them. You also can tap into the unseen world for informa-tion that will benefit and serve others.

If you are an 11/2 (almost all who have a 2 destiny are some form of an 11 (29=2+9=11 or 56=5+6=11), you want to become a "worker of the Light" who spreads your light on the path so others can be brought out of their own darkness. You are more sensitive than most people realize, and are very tuned in to the world from which you came. You have the ability to channel information for the world, and could become well known for your gifts. The 11/2 also can be an inspirational speaker, au-thor and actor. You want to be able to move people through these talents. Be patient if you are an 11. As in all Master Numbers, you are considered a late bloomer. It takes time and preparation for you to serve effec-tively.

If your full name totals to the number 3
(21, 30, 39, 48, 57, 66, 75, 84, 93, 102):

You want to become a very creative person in this lifetime. You want to know how to use your creative expression, particularly words, to bring joy and optimism to the world. You want to express cheerfulness and to help others lighten up. This can take you into many different fields of endeavor. Some with this destiny number go into the creative arts through painting, design, advertising, singing, acting and interior decorating. The strongest energy in the number 3 is always creative. You cannot hold this energy back in this lifetime. There must be a healthy release for it. For those who have this as a destiny number, you should find outlets to channel it. Many times, people who have predominant 3's in their charts but do **not** do any creative work develop diseases in the creative parts of their bodies, i.e., tumors in the uterus, cysts on the ovaries, prostate problems—areas of the body that are the source of creativity. Using your creative expression in the field of writing and speaking is one of the most common ways to channel this energy. Those who have this number as a destiny can make wonderful speakers and teachers. They have a certain wit about them, and can bring lightness to a dreary subject matter. A person with this destiny can help release the creative force of words by keeping a journal or a diary. Remember, sound moves energy. 3's are intimately involved with the words and, therefore, sounds. You are the creative force.

If your full name totals to the Number 4
(22, 31, 40, 49, 58, 67, 76, 85, 94, 103):

You desire to become a very productive and disciplined person in this lifetime. You are striving to become loyal, trustworthy, traditional, practical, results-oriented and methodical, and a person who brings form and structure to ideas. You do not want to be seen as lazy, and yet at the same time you want to keep a healthy balance between work and play. When others have great ideas, you want to see how those ideas can be formed to serve a practical function. Employment for a person who seeks a 4 destiny can be found in the building trades (lots of form and structure here), real estate (the number 4 rules real estate), the bookkeeper, the accountant, the orthopedic surgeon, the dentist, and all kinds of work that has great detail and structure.

You are learning in this lifetime to appreciate work, and you want others to see you as reliable and dependable. You may have had many past lives where you were wild and carefree, but in this lifetime you said you would acquire the above qualities to add to your Soul's knowledge. We need the 4 destiny people to help the rest of us gain a practical and productive structure to our daily lives. These people are considered the worker bees. If this is your destiny number, remember to maintain flexibility. This number can really box a person in to small-mindedness and a temptation to do things only a certain way. If that happens, it defeats the accomplishment. It also can make it very difficult for those around you. Flexibility and versatility are essential if you are to be successful in accomplishing this destiny.

If you are a 22/4 destiny, you are to become the Master Builder in this lifetime. This does not mean that you have to go into the building trades to accomplish your purpose. It means that you can choose an area based on your Learning Lesson and your Motivator and take that idea to its highest level. For example, perhaps you would like to be a teacher of children with special needs. If you have a Master Builder 22/4 destiny, you might want to build a center for these children and hire various teachers. This center could be a beacon for the world and an example of what can be done in that particular area. It is not unusual for those who have this number to be late bloomers and get the project started so that others can maintain and expand it even after you have gone back to the other side. Again, patience is essential. Preparation and grooming are a must.

If your full name totals to the Number 5
(23, 32, 41, 50, 59, 68, 77, 86, 95, 104):

You are striving to become an agent of change in this lifetime. It is essential that you learn how to handle freedom wisely and well. You want to become intimately close with what is involved with being truly free. A high level of freedom might be considered unconditional love. The extent to which you can learn this quality will be the gauge for the accomplishment of your destiny. It can take many forms. You can learn unconditional love by close personal relationships or through traveling the world and experiencing all kinds of unusual people and situations. Freedom will be essential for your growth and you will want to learn how to make change constructively. If you have a predominant 4 in your chart, you will always be torn between being practical, productive and hardworking, on the one hand, and being free. It's quite a predicament. If you can understand that the more disciplined you are the more freedom you will have, you can embrace both aspects.

Those who have this destiny can be found in professions that provide freedom of movement and time. Examples of this would be a lecturer, outside sales person, trainer, travel expert, promoter, teacher and preacher. From all your varied experiences you can use what you learned (including great stories) to help other people get unstuck and make constructive change in their lives. It all begins with you. It is important to use freedom wisely. This means raising the level of freedom out of the mundane and physical (sex, drugs, food, gambling, rock "n" roll) to the higher levels— freedom of the mind and a transference from the lower self to the higher self.

If your full name totals to the Number 6
(15, 24, 33, 42, 51, 60, 69, 78, 87, 96, 105):

You want to serve mankind in whatever direction your Life Path or Learning Lesson dictates. Your greatest desire is to accomplish something that helps others. It could be as simple as tutoring children to building a special hospice program for the dying. You want to become more loving, caring and helpful in this lifetime. If you do this in business, you might take it in the direction of having various programs that help your employees. Above all else, family and home traditions will be extremely important to you. You will do everything you can to try and protect them. You try to nurture others, and sometimes this will be shown by a love of cooking (food is important to this number) and entertaining in the home. You want to make the home the center of your life.

During this lifetime you may find that others rely on you a great deal. You want to be needed, so this does not faze you. In fact, it assists you in your desire to help and serve others. There is a healing quality about you, and others will seek you out for your ability to comfort. Be very careful that you do not interfere too much as there is a tendency to think that you know what is best for others. You do not want to put yourself into situations in which you don't belong. Since this number has the quality of two 3's in it, it is also highly creative. A 6 destiny can also be found in the art world. It is important to cultivate the artistic side of you if you have this as your destiny number. Because you possess a great deal of harmony, you make a great counselor and healer. The quality of harmony might also place you in the music world, either as a singer or a musician.

If you are a 33/6 destiny, you are even more of a universal helper. You will sacrifice even more to assist others. These people are usually found in professions where sacrifice is essential to carry out a plan. An example might be someone who takes a position that pays poorly but the position itself is essential for the good of others. The opportunity to serve the higher good for them is more important than the money that is made. These are truly your "Mother Teresa" types of individuals. You are the teacher of teachers. You are able to accept burdens placed upon you without resentment and complaints. You give your light so others may see. You might sacrifice creature comforts for the greater good. As with all 6 numbers, you have great artistic qualities that should be cultivated.

If your name totals to the Number 7
(25, 34, 43, 54, 61, 70, 79, 88, 97, 106):

You are striving to develop your higher mind and your higher self in this lifetime. This means that intellectual pursuits will be very important for your development. You should take every opportunity to expand your mind through increased knowledge, associate with people who spark your mind, and discipline yourself enough to pursue some course of study that will help you to become an expert or specialist in a particular field and develop faith over fear. It is a lifetime of schooling and receiving credentials and certificates. This lifetime would best be served by not just acquiring knowledge for knowledge's sake, but to really specialize and focus this knowledge, getting advanced degrees in a particular field so that people will seek you out for your specialty. Even if you are presently employed in a non-intellectual role, i.e., housecleaner, painter or cook, you will help yourself best if you find a way to enrich your mind in this lifetime. This can be done through part-time schooling until you can complete your course of study.

You also need to cultivate time in nature to appreciate the importance of the God force in all manifestations. You are acquiring a retiring, reflective quality in this lifetime, so time alone in nature is important for your growth. Meditation, contemplation, reflection are all things you are choosing to develop within yourself. It is not wise to be so busy that you do not have time for them. During this lifetime it is imperative that you strengthen your faith. A study of higher thought, religion, universal laws and manifestation should be part of your life. It is your Soul's plan to become in this lifetime an ethical person who uncovers and teaches the truth and is sought after by others for your sound and studious mind. You can make an excellent teacher. Some of the areas of interest to you are history, archeology, ancient religions, science, the environment, law, and philosophy. Be careful that you stay balanced between your heart and your head so that you don't just stay in the mind and become too critical and judgmental. Remember to specialize.

If your name totals to the Number 8
(26, 35, 44, 53, 62, 71, 80, 89, 98, 107):

You want to become an authority figure and leader in this lifetime. Therefore you should take every opportunity to practice positive leadership qualities. The benevolent leader is one who helps others become powerful through his or her own leadership and is not threatened by others' rise to power. As a leader you must learn to use your personal resources wisely. That means you most exercise wisdom in how you invest your energy, time and money. It is a waste-not, want-not destiny. It is always learning the laws of manifestation—how to create abundance and use it for its highest and best good; how to appreciate it and be grateful for what you have been given. In doing so you become a good example for others to follow. It is not about acquiring money, possessions and "stuff." Greed is not part of the equation, although the misuse of power and money can result in greed. You should cultivate strength and courage in this lifetime. It is imperative that you master yourself in the ways of the material world, as you have the potential to be a leader in whatever field you choose. Many with this destiny number go into the field of government, or become heads of companies, heads of churches and other organizations.

If you possess a 44/8 destiny, you should consider taking your leadership qualities into fields of work that help the world's underprivileged. You must work on developing a more intuitive side of yourself. You are strong in character, perseverance and courage but might be weak in the area of your intuition. Your Soul has chosen to cultivate this quality as part of its work during this lifetime. Learn to use and depend on the unseen world.

If your full name totals to the Number 9
(27, 36, 45, 54, 63, 72, 81, 90, 99, 108):

You want to become a humanitarian in this lifetime. Everything you do should take you toward development of this quality. Even if you have a position or company that is quite mundane or materialistic, you should cultivate your-self so that your work eventually benefits and serves humanity. If you are an artist, then teach painting to poor children or beautify the walls of a shelter. If you are the owner of an investment firm, set up a foundation so that part of your money and your friends' money can be directed to charitable causes. You said that in this lifetime you wanted to understand the human condition and to serve without worrying what was in it for you. You also wanted to learn the quality of detachment. It is, therefore, important that you not cling to things on this Earth. For example, if you depend on a certain person, a certain house, a certain neighborhood, a certain job or investment for your good, instead of relying on the unseen world from which you came, circumstances can be set up so that these things are removed from your life.

The teaching here is that you can use the things of this world, but do not depend on them. Since this number is considered to be a finishing number, you must learn to let go and remain detached. This does not mean that you cannot have wonderful relationships, great places to live, a wonderful spouse, etc. It means that you should not attach yourself to these things. You may use them but not "need" them. It means you must understand where your good comes from. In order to serve effectively, it is important that you develop detachment. You should not get too enmeshed in the emotional aspects of a person's dilemma. You can accomplish more to help and serve if you lean on the world of Spirit and not on the world of matter. You also are very prophetic and can see others in their full potential. It is important to learn to say "no" to people who continuously lean on you for your help. You do not want to make another person weak by your help.

Because this number has three aspects of the number 3 within it (3x3=9), it is the ultimate in beauty. We use the phrase "dressed to the nines" as the mark of taste and refinement. This is a very sensitive, artistic vibration, and those who carry this number should be involved in some aspect of the creative world. For example, if the Life Path or Life Lesson was the number 5 and the catalyst of change and the destiny was the number 9, that person could teach people how to make effective change in their lives in such a way that empowers them. If the Life Path or Learning Lesson was the number 3, the creative number, the individual might write books or articles that would inspire people to help themselves and be more positive about their lives.

ဢ *Chapter 11* os

Your Karmic Corrections
for this Lifetime

"We live our life again:
Or warmly touched or coldly dim
The pictures of the Past remain,
Man's works shall follow him:"
—*John Greenleaf Whittier, American poet*

We hear the word "karma" used loosely in our society. Do you have good karma? Bad karma? Do you have *any* karma? The word definitely conjures up more fear than faith. There is also the fatalist's viewpoint that it must be your karma to go through such and such an event. Maybe and maybe not. How's that for a reasonable answer?

Karma is not complicated. Some of it we created in this lifetime and some of it in prior lives. What is it? It's balance. If we keep in mind that the Universe is in a Divine Order (Remember, the Bible tells you that "your days are numbered," and there is even a book in the Bible called "Numbers"), we always know then that everything must be kept in balance. So if I decide to cheat someone out of his or her money, sooner or later I will be cheated out of a similar amount. The pay back might not come from the person I cheated. It might come in a parking ticket for that particular amount. It does keep everything in balance, though, doesn't it?

Let me tell you a story. Many years ago a client told me what happened to him after he didn't pay a restaurant bill. It seems it was a very busy Saturday night and he and his date for the evening kept asking for the bill at a restaurant in Los Angeles. After a frustrating period, they decided to walk out, obviously not paying the bill. He told me they went only a few blocks in their car and stopped at a stop sign. Within minutes after they left the stop sign, they were stopped by the police, who said they didn't make a complete stop. The driver, of course, insisted that he had, but he was given the ticket anyway. The amount of the ticket was almost the exact same amount as the dinner he hadn't paid. Now that is swift karma.

Not all karma is that obvious or that swift. It is easier to understand present day events when we can connect them to activities we know we did or should not have done. It is more difficult to understand events that happen when we see no reason for the experience. We try to explain it away by saying it is God's will or fate. My belief is that God or Infinite Being is a loving energy that does not wish to punish us. This loving energy gave us free will to choose how to think and make decisions from these choices. Now, if they were the wrong choices, that was our free will choice. We have the opportunity to experience the results of these choices. Many of these choices were made long ago, not in this lifetime. It can be said, then, that we also choose which choices from past lives we will balance out and correct in this lifetime. *Nobody did anything to us.* We did it all to ourselves. Many of the most difficult situations we find ourselves in are the result of our misguided and negative deeds from prior lives. It is my belief that what we call "bad things happening to good people" is a result of past life behavior. Certainly if I associate with "persons of ill repute" in this lifetime I will probably find myself in unpleasant situations. It was my free will choice to associate with them; nobody made me do it.

This brings me to the point of looking at this life to see what, if any, karma you are working out from prior lives. Clues for this information are located in your birth name. You can easily tell which karmic lessons are being activated by seeing which numbers are missing in your name. If all the letters in your name represent one of the numbers 1 through 9, there is no particular karmic lesson carried forward. **That doesn't mean you don't have lessons to learn or issues with self-development** It just means that during this particular lifetime you are not carrying much imbalance in your life. You have the choice to maintain this balance or create new imbalances. You have reached a point of your growth where there is much harmony.

Study your name again and, using the letters and corresponding numbers in Figure c, list what letters are missing. Now see what numbers correspond to these letters. These missing numbers in your name signify your karmic corrections for this life.

Missing Numbers

If you are missing the number 1 (no a, j or s)

You are to learn to be more independent, self-directed, self-reliant, assertive, original, courageous, innovative, and willful. You should avoid being too stubborn, indecisive, selfish and passive. This missing number indicates that in past lives you avoided taking the leadership role, or you may have overdone that role. You are given a chance in this lifetime to practice being a leader and taking charge. You will be forced to speak up for your opinions and assert your will.

If you are missing the number 2 (no b, k or t)

You are to learn to be more patient, cooperative, diplomatic, persuasive instead of forceful, a team player, and sensitive to the effect your will has on others. You should avoid being super-sensitive and taking everything personally. Watch the tendency toward gossip and hoarding— never throwing anything away. This missing number indicates past lives where you did many things on your own or without a partner. There is a strong need to experience what it is like to be in a partnership, especially the give and take of a partnership. Learn patience and the ability to compromise. Don't force your will on others.

If you are missing the number 3 (no c, l or u)
You have a tendency to be very hard on yourself. You have set an impossible standard that nobody could live up to. You need to lighten up on yourself, be more positive, cheerful and optimistic. Learn the value of words, both spoken and written, and develop your creative talents. If this number is missing in your name, it can indicate past lives where you did not appreciate your creative gifts. Refine your appearance. Be careful of meaningless chatter, talking too much, a scattering of your energy and a reluctance to draw attention to yourself. It is helpful with this missing number to pay attention to your posture; there can be a tendency to slouch.

If you are missing the number 4 (no d, m or v)
You need to learn to value work and discipline. There is an indication from past lives that work was not appreciated or was devalued by you. In this lifetime you will have to work hard for what you hope to accomplish. There is a need for order, structure and a methodical approach to life. No get-rich-quick schemes in this lifetime. The more disciplined you become, the easier your life will work. Avoid rigidity, narrow-mindedness and penny-pinching. There might be a tendency to change jobs regularly thinking that a new job will be the answer. However, after the new job begins you will find that the same complaints crop up. Embrace order and work in your life and your life will run smoothly.

If you are missing the number 5 (no e, n or w)

You must learn to be flexible and able to embrace change. There is a need to let go of the old and take risks without knowing all the facts. Change will be forced on you in this lifetime, so that you will get unstuck. You will be faced with various opportunities to change creating stress and pressure until you become more versatile and less fearful of change. It is an opportunity to experience freedom in this lifetime and not get stuck in safe, secure positions. This indicates that in past lives you had little freedom or were too rigid.

If you are missing the number 6 (no f, o or x)

You must learn to be more responsible and committed. Life will put you into positions where you will have to be responsible for family members and coworkers. This missing number indicates that in past lives you avoided the domestic scene, marriage, children and family. In this lifetime you may find you are the sole breadwinner in the family or you may again skip the idea of any children at all. This number also indicates that you have an issue with commitment. You might create relationships where the other person appears not to be able to commit to you. You also might not finish all that you start. Be aware of your tendency to stay heavily guarded in close personal relationships. The other person might feel you do not really care, as they do not feel your affection and caring. This missing number indicates a bumpy road in marriage and a challenge to you to learn to be sincere in your relationships.

If you are missing the number 7 (no g, p or y)

You have avoided the development of your higher mind or you overdid it, meaning that you operated strictly out of your head without feelings. There is a need to learn discernment in this lifetime. Do not take things at face value. Learn to question and to focus on a subject matter in depth. It is a lifetime to avoid superficial knowledge. An excellent opportunity to go to school and receive advanced degrees. You should specialize. With this missing number you will be instructed in the development of faith over fear. You must strengthen your faith. Investigate, reflect and meditate. Get in touch with your Spiritual self. Do not be afraid to spend time alone in contemplation. Welcome mental pursuits and avoid emotional decisions. Use your reasoning power to help you.

If you are missing the Number 8 (no h, q or z)

You must learn to use your resources wisely. The most prevalent resources are your time, energy and money. You are also learning to use your power and authority wisely. You will be taught the limits of your resources until you learn this lesson. Most likely you will enter this lifetime thinking you know everything. In the beginning it will be hard to tell you anything as you will see advice as criticism. You might always think you can do everything better than the person in charge. This usually comes from past lives where you avoided or abused your power. In this lifetime you are being instructed in the correct use, and not abuse, of power. Use common sense in all your dealings, be honest with your business dealings and avoid manipulating and controlling others.

If you are missing the Number 9 (no i or r)

You must learn to be more of a humanitarian. You should practice compassion, tolerance, unconditional love and concern for others without expectation of getting anything back. This is important to remember. You should avoid giving to get, or for the sake of manipulating others. Do more charity work if this is one of your missing numbers. You are to learn to be more detached and forgiving. It would be wise to also develop an appreciation for art and beauty.

❧ *Chapter 12* ❧

The Wise Plan

"Choose always the way that seems right; however rough it may be. Practice will make it easy and pleasant."
—Pythagoras

If you have planned wisely for this lifetime, you most likely will have created a Personality number, a Motivating number, a Destiny number or your Life Path number that corresponds to one or more of your karmic corrections. One of my clients has a remarkable plan. In her name she was missing the numbers 4, 6 and 7. When I read her Personality number (her consonants), it totaled to a 7. When I read her Motivating Number or Soul Number (her vowels), it totaled to a 6. When I read her Destiny number (the total of her full name), it totaled to a 4. Her Soul had planned to use each of her karmic corrections numbers as one or more of her directions for this life. By doing this she had simplified her karma. What that means is, her personality by being the Number 7 would operate as the quality of 7. She would then literally behave and think as this vibration. Her Soul number, by being the 6, would be motivated to come from a place of that quality. Her Destiny, by being the 4, would push her to try and achieve that quality during her whole life. She is actually helping herself balance out all the karmic corrections she had brought with her into this lifetime. If one of your missing numbers is your Life Path or Learning Lesson, the correction will be the focus or essence of your life and easy to correct.

What if there are no missing numbers?

This question comes up periodically if a person has at least one of all the numbers in their name. Does this mean there is no karma awaiting this person? No. This individual has chosen not to work with that karma during this particular life. He or she may be postponing the karma in order to concentrate only on a Destiny or Life Path lesson. As explained earlier, life is meant to be in balance. The trick is to maintain harmony. This is definitely challenging.

How do you behave so you do not create more karma for yourself? It is not unusual for those who have this situation in this lifetime to feel as if the entire time here is somewhat less than thrilling. Many times I am asked by these Souls why they are really here. It "feels" like they have done all this before. These individuals have definitely spent many lives on the Earth plane. Most of the experiences that happen to us have happened many times over to these individuals. They seem to have more of a detachment to being here. Their response to difficult situations may appear calmer than the average person's response. I have a client who has this situation. She is not missing any numbers in her chart. She has plenty of money to do whatever she wants to do, but she would rather stay at home, tend her garden, read and do simple activities rather than take a trip around the world or eat meals at the finest restaurant. She can take it or leave it. If she goes, fine, if she doesn't go, it's not a big deal. The feeling is much like "Been there, done that." This is also true in the way one of these individuals would respond to emergency situations.

While all those around them might be hysterical, the person with no missing numbers will be calmly dialing 911 or keeping everyone else from falling apart. It is interesting to watch.

What if you have an abundance of a particular number?

This signifies a propensity toward that quality. Remember, your name is a clear indication of what experiences you have been a part of in past lives. If there are missing numbers, there is an imbalance in those qualities—usually not enough of that energy. If there is an excessive amount, you have gone overboard in that area. For instance, one time I did a reading for an individual who had ten 1's in her name. It was loaded with the letters "a" and "s." My goodness this woman was independent and bossy. She had to be the leader in everything. She tried to run other people's meetings as well as control speakers through her questions. She had to be Number One.

Someone who had more than three 4's in her or his name would be too work- oriented and would have to try to make change more easily. That person could be very stubborn and believe things should always be done a certain way. Another person had eight 5's in her name. That person had a very hard time disciplining herself. She didn't particularly like work, and it showed in her chart that she had karma in the area of the Number 4. This would be a lifetime for her of trying to become more disciplined and methodical. The customary number of 1's would be approximately two or three, not ten. It is normal to have two of each letter. If you have three or more, you have more than the average. The exception is the number 5. This is the most common number in the Western world (e, n and w). The average of four or five of these is normal. The other exception is the Number 7. It is very normal to have this number missing in your name (no g, p or y). The missing Number 7 always is a test of Faith over Fear. Many of the reincarnated Souls on this planet are experiencing the lack of this energy.

In the past Piscean Age (approximately the last 2,400 years), it was not unusual for someone to separate from humanity to learn religious and spiritual teachings. Many of those who chose to do this had to go away from the masses and live lives of solitude, seclusion and silence. Many of those on the Earth plane did not want to do this. Since we have left that age and are now in the Age of Aquarius, we can learn religious and spiritual teachings WITH humanity. We do not have to separate ourselves. We can attend classes, workshops and lectures. We can buy and discuss books. We can try on various forms of religious teachings, all in the context of friends and strangers. We no longer have to use the "begging bowl" or cloister ourselves to learn. Now, we can still do that if we choose, but there are more than enough group activities to learn these teachings without the sacrifice of the self. Since it is more comfortable to learn in this manner, Souls have brought this karmic correction in with them to balance it out in this lifetime.

∾ *Chapter 13* ∽

Your Time Frames

"The years teach much that the days never know."
—Emerson

In addition to the information located in the name at birth, there is also information located in the date of birth. This information tells you of your particular time frames. Remember, I said earlier that we each have our own time frames. You are not on anyone else's time. I also mentioned that a blueprint is approximately 120 years. You have customized your time here so that you will be focusing on particular experiences. Now we think we must accomplish certain milestones based on man-made laws and cultural traditions. These, however, are always changing. Even the age of retirement and Social Security programs keeps changing. We didn't even have retirement programs at the start of the 20th century. Beneath all these artificial time frames lies your own personal time frame. Once you know this, you can concentrate on your own growth based on your Divine Timetable.

Understanding Your Pinnacles

During the Soul's Earth life, there will be a total of four time frames, also known as **Pinnacles**. Each will last a certain number of years. You must use your Life Path number to see at what age you will activate them and how long they will last.

You begin to calculate your first Pinnacle by working with the number 36. This number is actually four cycles of the number 9. 4 x 9 = 36. From this number, 36 years, you deduct the number of your Life Path (the sum total of your date of birth). For instance, if your Life Path totaled to the number 5, you would deduct 5 from 36 or 36 - 5 = 31. Your first Pinnacle would be 31 years long.

To calculate your second Pinnacle, add the number 9 to the number at the end of the first Pinnacle. In this case the second Pinnacle would last from age 32 through age 40 years (a total of nine years).

To calculate the third Pinnacle, add the number 9 to the number at the end of the second Pinnacle. In this case the third Pinnacle would last from age 41 through age 49 (again, a total of nine years).

The fourth Pinnacle begins at the next year after completion of the third Pinnacle. In this case it would be from the age of 50. The fourth Pinnacle stays with you from this time forward. It is your last Pinnacle. See figure c.

When one of these time frames is activated, everything can change. We can go from being a hermit to a very active lifestyle, or vice versa. We can go from a charmed life to a time frame that activates a karmic correction. These Pinnacles give us our timetables. You can see that a person could be in a Pinnacle for a number of years and never think that things will change. You can be encouraged or discouraged, but you will change. Remember, generally speaking, we are more effective after we reach 50, or the Soul Cycles of 7 years times 7. We really know ourselves better, have enough Earth experience and can be more authentic in what our needs are after the age of 50. This is certainly a far cry from our man made society that emphasizes youth and material success by the age of 40.

Each of these Pinnacles is marked by the numeric vibration 1 through 9. Your date of birth dictates which number you will activate. It can be compared to being in a particular class of instruction for many years. You have been focusing for all those years on the particular instruction for that class. At a certain age you activate one of these Pinnacles and move to a different class. This is why so many people are shocked when their lives, which have been going in one direction, suddenly change. They may not want the same job. They may want to go to school, travel, take care of others, have a family, goof off, and a variety of other experiences. It is best to remember that you maintain your Life Path, your Personality, your Destiny and your Motivator or Heart's Desire throughout these time periods. _If one of these Pinnacles is the same as one of these numbers or one of your karmic corrections, its meaning will be even more accentuated in your life._

To learn which number you are activating at these different ages, we must use simple calculations using your month, day and year of birth. We will use the birthday of October 10, 1941 for our example.

> Your first Pinnacle is found by adding your **month** of birth to your **day** of birth and reducing this to a single number.
> For example, if your birth month is October (10th month) and your birth day is 28, you would add 10 + 28 = 38. Add 3 + 8 = 11. Add 1 + 1 = 2. In this example your first Pinnacle would be 11 or a 2.

> Your second Pinnacle is found by adding your **day** of birth to your **year** of birth. If your day of birth is 28 and your year of birth is 1941, you would add 28 to 1 + 9 + 4 + 1 = 15. Adding 28 to 15 totals 43. 4 + 3 = 7. Your second Pinnacle

would be 7.

Your third Pinnacle is found by **adding the previous two** Pinnacles together. 2 + 7 = 9. Your third Pinnacle would be 9.

Your fourth Pinnacle is found by adding the **month** to the **year.** You would add 10 to 1941 or 10 + (1+9+4+1 = 15). 10 + 15 would be 25. 2 + 5 = 7. Your fourth Pinnacle would be 7.

Figure (c)

William Jefferson Blythe (the real birth name of Bill Clinton) born August 19, 1946, or 8-19-20 (1+9+4+6=20)

Life Path = 11/2 (8+19+20=47 (4+7=11/2)

Pinnacle #1

Subtract 2 from 36= 34 years
Pinnacle #1 will be a "9"
8 + 19 = 27 (2 + 7=9)
From age 0 (birth) through age 34 the Pinnacle will be 27 or a 9 (2+7)

Pinnacle #2

Add 9 years to the last Pinnacle
Pinnacle #2 will be a "3"
19 + 20 = 39 (3 + 9 = 3)
From age 35 through age 43 the Pinnacle will be 39 or a 3 (3+9)

Pinnacle# 3

Add 9 years to the last Pinnacle
Pinnacle #3 will be a "3"
From age 44 through age 52 the Pinnacle will be 9 + 3 = 12 or 1 + 2 = 3
(We add the first two Pinnacles together)

Pinnacle #4 (the final)

Pinnacle lasts from the age when the third Pinnacle ended to the end of the life.) Add the year of birth to the month of birth.

From age 53 to the completion of his life the Pinnacle will be 20 (1+9+4+6=20) added to Bill Clinton's month of August (8ᵗʰ month). 8 + 20 = 28. 2 + 8 = 10. 1+ 0 = 1
Clinton's final Pinnacle will be Number 1.

Each one of these Pinnacles has specific meaning for you. Remember to reduce the totals to a single digit.

Pinnacle 1

During this time frame you will be instructed in the correct use of your will. This is a period of time in which you must be willing to gain confidence and do things without waiting for someone else to do them with you or for you. You must learn to be initiating, more courageous and independent. For whatever reasons, your Soul has said it wants this experience. It could mean that in prior lives you were too independent, and willful and during this period of your life you can learn how to be independent without being overly willful. If you are missing the number 1 in your name, this would be a very important time, during this particular lifetime, to learn this lesson. The karmic correction would be activated during these ages. Normally a Soul would create this experience because there is a need to use the will wisely and eventually learn to co-create your human will with your Divine Will. Above all else, be initiating and innovative.

Pinnacle 2

During this time frame you must be patient, diplomatic, compromising, tactful and work closely with others. This is not a time to push your way or be too dogmatic. Patience is essential during this period. If you insist on having your own way, things can implode on you and you will find yourself not getting what you wanted. You are being asked to be diplomatic and to use persuasion rather than force during this period. You will find yourself in partnership situations, and may find that your work environment requires you to work with someone you distinctly dislike. If you are a headstrong individual, this period will be extremely challenging. Be a team player, and above all else be patient. Force does not work during this period.

Pinnacle 3

You are being asked to use your creative talent during this period as well as to be joyful and optimistic. This is normally a very pleasant period, and things can be much easier. The downside of this period is that if things get too easy you could become complacent and not accomplish much during it. Many people who arrive at this Pinnacle in their charts have a tendency to goof off. They try on several different activities and squander the time. This period will bring out your creative side. It is imperative that you focus on a particular area of your creativity and enhance it. Do not scatter yourself into trivial pursuits. Do not become the painter, the singer, the designer, the photographer and tap dancer. Choose one area and really focus on it. If it is writing, write. But write to get published. Really focus your creative energy. If you are missing the number 3 in your name (c, l or u), use this period to really overcome your self-critical nature. Push yourself to be heard, to be imaginative, creative, joyful and optimistic.

Pinnacle 4

During this period you will dig your heels in and work. It is a time for foundation laying. You will be working hard. It is also a time to be practical with all your affairs. Most of your vacation time will be short and somehow connected to your work. The good side about this period of your life is that you are setting yourself up for results and rewards. This is the preparatory period. Be very careful that you don't get out of balance and do nothing but work during this period. Remember to play and to stay flexible. You can accomplish quite a bit at this time, but you can also wear yourself out. This time frame can be the workaholic years of your life.

It is during this period that your family needs will be met in a more material way. You will be working to produce the income to pay for their needs. If you have a karmic correction of the number 4 (no d, m or v), this period could be very challenging. You will have to be very practical and discipline yourself. You may find yourself having to take jobs you dislike so that you remain employed. Your Soul has said it wants this experience. Remember, the ego/personality may or may not like it. It depends on what numbers are in your individual chart. This is a fairly difficult first pinnacle. If it is your first pinnacle, you may find yourself going to work at a very early age. If it is your last pinnacle, you will be productive right up to the time you depart for your return home.

Pinnacle 5

During this period you will come to know the true use of freedom. There will be many unexpected changes. You will have to get used to change and learn how to make constructive change. The temptation during this period is to become a rolling stone. Be careful. You will need to ground yourself in a career or relationship so that you will gain its benefits. Do not think that the career or relationship will stifle you. It will give you a base from which you can make change and actually have more freedom. True freedom is "unconditional love." It is during this period that you will come to know what that really means. It is a time of self-promotion and progress. If you have gotten stuck in your life, this is the time to make wise changes. There will be a tendency during this period to get bored with what you are

doing. Be careful that all changes have been preceded by reflection and analysis.

A temptation during this period is also to experiment too
much with sensual delights. Since the number 5 rules the five
senses, there can be an over-indulgence in too much of the world.
Be discerning in thoughts of sexual liaisons and the tendencies to
gamble, drink or have freedom at any cost. This period, like any
other period, can create great disharmony in your Soul's growth
if it is not handled wisely. Life will be your teacher. You will
travel more and experience many different kinds of people and
situations during this period. Remember, the more disciplined you
become, the more freedom you will have.

Pinnacle 6

This period of your life will teach you much about your responsibility for others, particularly in the family. You will find
yourself needed more by others and caring for them in nourishing
ways. It is at this time period that the family becomes your
teacher. If you have karma in commitment, responsibility for
others and showing your true affection and caring, this is one of
the most challenging times of your lives. You will not be able to
get out from underneath this teaching. It is during this period
that everybody seems to need a piece of you. Be careful that you
do not allow yourself to become a doormat or to meddle where
you do not belong. The positive aspect of this time period is that
you will be greatly loved and needed. Your community service
time is here. What can you do to help? Since the number 6 is a
very creative and harmonious number, you could also increase
your creativity during this time frame. Paint, sing, write and
express these aspects of yourself. There will be many adjustments in the home during this period: births, graduations, children leaving the home and all activities around these events.
Enjoy them. It is a good feeling to be loved and appreciated.

Pinnacle 7

This is a great period of rest, recuperation and reflection. It is an excellent time to go to school to perfect your knowledge and your expertise. Your inner world is now active. It is actually not a business period so don't try to push things in that direction. It is a time period in which you are developing your mind and your higher knowledge. You have arranged this time frame to develop the inner part of you, not your outside world. Of course, when we develop our inner self, all kinds of changes take place in the outer world. It is at this time of your life that you will need more time alone. If your family members feel insecure about your need to be alone more, explain to them that it is not them but your own need to have time to contemplate, study and figure things out. You are developing you, the higher aspect of you. This is important work. You are developing your intuition. Once you come to depend on your intuition, you will find that it will be your guide and your life can be much easier. Of course, if this pinnacle activates a missing number 7 in your chart (no g, p or y), you will find it more challenging to go within and concentrate on your inner world. It is at this time that the lesson of Faith over Fear will be taught. Develop your faith. It is what your Soul has requested.

Pinnacle 8

At this time of your life you are dealing with the material world. Even if you don't want to, you will be pushed to handle your money, your time and your energy very wisely. You will have to learn to work with your personal authority and to make every effort to become successful. This is an excellent period for success, but it requires you to be courageous and strong. It is a "waste not, want not" period. You will use your resources very wisely. I call this period your harvest period, because you can accomplish so much during it. Be careful that you do not become lost in power, money and greed. You are being instructed in the correct use, and not abuse, of your power. Do not use money or power as your god or it will do you in. If this is one of your karmic correction numbers (no h, q or z), be very careful that you understand the Spiritual principles of abundance. You must learn to use the Spiritual in the material world. There will be a tendency to just want to make money and be the boss. Watch out. The Universe has an elegant way of waiting and waiting until the invisible world of Spirit pulls you in. You can be successful during this period but it must be done with high intentions. During this period, become the benevolent leader. The benevolent leader helps others become successful as well.

Pinnacle 9

During this period you will be given the opportunity to be of service to humanity, to learn more about the human condition, to learn to let go, develop detachment and to work with your creative talents. You may experience mini births and deaths during this period. These are not actual physical deaths, but a form of death in the letting go of people and plans. You will be given the opportunity to learn what others need, and how you can help them but without getting too deeply involved. Sometimes there is an element of sacrifice attached to this. It depends on the situation. Since this is such a highly creative period, it is a wonderful time to get involved with the arts. You could become a benefactor or patron of the arts. Any work or project you attach yourself to that benefits and serves humanity will be very successful for you. You will learn during this period that you can attach yourself to the unseen world for your good. You can use the material world, but do not depend upon it. At this period of your life you are putting good deposits in your karma bank. Make sure you do something that helps your fellow humans. If you are missing this number in your name (no i or r), this is your golden opportunity to give of yourself to help others. Your Soul has created this time period to activate opportunities to be of service.

Your Personal Year

Each of us not only has Pinnacles in our lives but also has a Personal Year. Your Personal Year is your individual energy for the year. Remember, I spoke earlier about timing. We should know our own timing so that we can begin projects or end projects at the right time. One of the biggest losses on the Earth plane is a lack of awareness of our own Personal Year. It very important to understand and work with your personal time frame. Your Personal Year is found by simply adding the month of your birth to the date of your birth to the Universal Year. What is the Universal Year? It is the year you are living in today. For example, 2001 is a 3 Universal Year. 2002 is a 4 Universal Year. 2003 is a 5 Universal year. We derive the Universal Year by adding the year together. 2+0+0+1=3, 2+0+0+2=4, 2+0+0+3=5.

If your birthday is February 10, you would add 2 (February is the 2nd month) to 10 (the day) to 3 (the Universal Year for 2001). Your Personal Year would be 6. 2+1+0+3=6. See Figure d.

Figure (d)

Month = 2   Day =10
Universal Year = 3   (2 + 0 + 0 + 1 = 3)
Your Personal Year = 15 Add together 1 + 5 = 6

It is important to remember that a Personal Year begins January 1 of each year. It does not start on your birthday. However, you will be experiencing stronger qualities of the year *the closer you get to your actual birthday.* Keep in mind that the first two months of each year, January and February, are always involved with the energy of the old year. You really don't get things moving forward until March or April. You will also see more of the energy consolidating as you get into the fall and end of a year.

Personal Year 1

This is your seed-planting year, the year to begin new projects, new jobs, new location and in general a fresh start. It is a year of new beginnings. If there is anything you need to clean up from the previous year, try to do it early in the year. You want to use most of the energy from this year to start new endeavors. Seed wisely this year, as the garden will last a long time. Much of what you harvest eight years from now will be the result of what you planted during this year. It is extremely important. Don't be lazy about your life. Be aware of new people you meet—even though they may seem to be just a passing interlude. You are preparing your garden. Don't wait for somebody to do it with you. It is a year to take risks, be courageous and take care of what you need to do. Take the initiative. Do not expect the plans to be completed in this year. You are just getting started. It is not a particularly good year for partnerships. You need to do many things on your own and devote time and energy to getting your plans started. You will have plenty of time next year for relationships.

Personal Year 2

This is the year for patience, diplomacy, partnerships and teamwork. Patience is essential. All the plans you started last year are now growing roots. You need to tend the garden. So much of what you started needs work and refinement. This can be a year of delays, as you must work with others and wait on them for many of your decisions. If you try to force your own way this year, it will not work. You will find yourself frustrated and may lose some friendships and/or relationships because you pushed

too hard. There may be a natural end of some of your relationships in July of this year. You will feel more sensitive this year
and will not want to be alone as you were last year. It is an
excellent year for relationships, particularly an important love
relationship. In August you will begin to solidify your efforts, and
by fall much of what gave you frustration will be resolved. I urge
you to keep your plans to yourself this year. You have certain
hopes, wishes and dreams, but they need time to root themselves. If you divulge your plans to others, you risk the chance of
their being blown away or delayed. Keep your secrets.

Personal Year 3

This is a year of expansion and creativity. A very good year
to expand your efforts and promote the plans you made in your
1 year. It is a highly creative year, so I encourage you to choose
an area of expression that you love and focus on it this year.
Really make an effort to use your imagination. Concentrate on
the ideas and inspirations that you planted in your 1 year. It is a
wonderful year to make new friends and improve your appearance. Change your hairstyle, change your clothes and do everything you can to present yourself as being attractive. Your net-
working will pay off. Make contacts and socialize. Create a new
business card. This can be a good financial year if you do your
work. Do not drift along. The wind is at your back, and if you
concentrate on your creative project you will do well. Consider
travel this year.

Personal Year 4

This is the year you roll up your sleeves and work. The plans
you made in the last few years have been expanding. Now they
need structure, so they will have concrete form. This is a year to
be very practical and industrious. It is not a year to take long
vacations. You have work to do and it will be the focus of this

year. It is also not a year to change jobs or move. Wait until next year if you can. If you change jobs, be very cautious. Make sure the job is what it appears to be. It is not a year to be unemployed. I consider this to be a contracted year rather than an expansive year. If you make a move this year, the wind is in your face. It is better if you make all the changes next year. You are actually laying the foundation for future years. This can be a very rewarding year, but only if you have put in the effort. Your finances may seem slow in materializing. You may have more expenses than you expected. During this year, keep your overhead low and postpone unnecessary purchases until next year when your finances will improve. Pace yourself, as you may find yourself working very hard this year. You need this year to make sure your plans can be implemented.

Personal Year 5

Okay, this is the year to make the changes you have been waiting for. Five can be a pretty nerve-wracking year, as there is so much change going on. Just when you think you are going north, you are going south. The change continues until about October, when things begin to solidify. It is very important to take the opportunity this year to promote and market yourself. It is not a year to stay stuck. Make changes in your career, your location, your thinking and embrace change in general. Pay attention to clues on your path. Someone may say something or give you needed information about an opportunity in your life. This is the time to make decisions without knowing all the facts. It will take courage, but there are many opportunities at this time. Be careful how you make change this year. You do not want to leave chaos behind. Evaluate your situation. Look at the situation you have gotten yourself into and make the appropriate changes to balance your life.

This year can also be a "sexy" year. If you are single, it is a year to date and socialize. Be careful that you do not overindulge in the physical plane. Five rules the five senses. Watch out for too much drinking, food, sex, drugs, and rock "n" roll. Be very wise. It is a great year to travel so get out there and enjoy yourself. Above all don't be overly cautious. You are shedding the heavy restrictions from the last four years.

Personal Year 6

This is the year of family and domestic responsibility. You will be needed a great deal by others, and may find yourself many times feeling burdened by the responsibility. Not to worry—this is a golden opportunity for you to be of service to others and to assist where you can. You will feel loved and needed this year. There is also a "luck" factor regarding this number, so you may find good opportunities in your business and financial areas. The year is very busy. You will have to pace yourself so that you don't get exhausted from your responsibilities. An interesting characteristic about this year is that it can bring a change in your eating habits. There is usually a change to a healthier eating pattern. You will be doing things that improve your health.

Another characteristic of a 6 year is an improvement in your home. During a 6 year you might fix up your existing home, add an addition or even move to a better home. It's a very loving year, you will feel more appreciated, needed and might even find yourself getting married. Because the number six is the number of marriage and family, there are many adjustments made in those areas during this year. It could be a marriage (or a divorce), the birth of a child or the releasing of a child that goes off to college—all involved with love, family, commitment and the home.

Personal Year 7

After all the responsibility of the 6 year, all the changes of the 5 year, the work of the 4 year, the new creations of the 3 year, the planning and patience of the 2 year and the planting and innovation of the 1 year, you have earned a rest. Here it is. This year is intended to be a sabbatical year, a time of rest, recovery, reflection and planning. It is not a year to be very active in the outer world. It is a year in which you will develop your higher mind and your higher self. You may feel very tired this year. Don't worry—that feeling is needed so that you will slow down and take it easy. You have been charging forward for six years. Everything is to rest in this important seven year. Nature rests every seven years. We as a population are to rest on the seventh day. Keep this in mind. You will not have this opportunity to rest for a long time.

You also need this year to plan your future activities. If you are rushing around in your old pattern of work and activities, you will not have time to think things through. Take time out to do that. Cut back your work hours, spend time in nature, take some classes of higher learning, improve your skills, study Spiritual teachings, develop the higher mind and pay attention to the "self". I once told a woman that she should take it easy in her 7 year and postpone her move if possible to the next year, which was only three months away. She was insistent on moving. During the move, she broke her ankle and went through an "enforced rest" for several months.

This is a year to be selfish. Your future actions will be based on well-thought plans. If you don't take the time to do this, you could possibly make many mistakes in your decisions in the years to come. You will come to a head in your decisions, so this year may feel like a door is closing. It is. You will not, however, end this cycle of time until two years from now. Once you complete a 7 year, the 8 and 9 years will be used to complete the cycle.

This is not a beginning year. You are actually winding this cycle down.

Personal Year 8

This is your harvest year. If you have planned well in your 7 year, you know what you need to do. Remember the seeds you planted in your 1 year? These were the risks you took, the new job you started and the new business you created. Now is the time to reap what you have sowed. It is a great year to go after what you want. Do not be shy. Knock on doors you would previously have been reluctant to open. This is the time when all you have done pays off. That is why it is so important to plant wisely in a 1 year. Last year, in your 7 year, you were mainly concerned with the self and probably didn't experience very much on the material plane. That can change this year. This is the year when you can get that big contract, the job promotion and other material successes. As dry and lonely as the 7 year might have been, this year is the opposite. You can be ambitious, forceful and more confident. It's the year to bring home the rewards. Be focused and pursue your goals. If you spent time in your 7 year on your plans, then you know what to do.

If you have not put in the effort over the last seven years, this can be a year of meager return. All results are in direct proportion to the effort you have put in during the last seven years. You could have large expenses connected to making money this year, so be very efficient with your resources. Remember resources are not just money. They are time, energy and money.

Personal Year 9

This is your year of completion, endings and letting go. You are finishing up a nine-year cycle. It is a year to discard the old to make way for the new next year. During this year you may feel that you need to get rid of old clothing and clean out the cobwebs of your life. There is a general trend throughout the year of finishing up unfinished business. You may have debts still to be paid; take care of them this year. You may be contemplating the end of a relationship or a job. This is also the year when chronic illnesses may end. Do not cling to things that want to leave your life. This is where the year can be very painful. It is a letting-go year, and when something or someone wants to leave your life, you should let them go. If a relationship was a strain or a job unfulfilling, do you really want to carry them forward in your life? In order to make room for the new that is coming next year, you must clean out to create a fresh space.

In addition to completing things in this year, it is a year of charitable service. Spend part of this year in compassionate work for humanity. You get to choose which area to serve, but try to fit it in. This is not work you get paid for. It is giving of yourself freely without worrying about what is in it for you. Another area of interest this year is in the arts. Your creativity is very high this year. You may find yourself doing sculpturing or photography. Enjoy this aspect of the year. Be courageous. Letting go can be painful, but remember, you have a brand new exciting year coming. By October and November you will be anxious to have it begin. Make good use of this year, mourn your losses if you need to and then remember the new dawn that is just ahead.

Your Personal Month or Day

Within your personal year there are also personal months and days. It is helpful to know the personal month, but less important to know the personal day. The personal year is the most important time frame; the personal month has less importance and the personal day even less. They all, however, present you with a guide that can keep you on course.

To discover your **Personal Month**, add the single digit of the month to your Personal Year Number. If you are in a 2 Personal

Year and are in the month of February (a 2 month), you would add the 2 of the Personal Year to the 2 of the month. February would then be your Personal Month of 4. March would then be a Personal Month of 5, April a Personal Month of 6 and May a Personal Month of 7.

To discover your **Personal Day** add the number of the day in the month to your Personal Month. When you total a compound number or two digits, also reduce it to a single digit. For example if you are in a 4 Personal Month and it is the 14th day of that month, you would add the 2 Personal Month to the number 5 (14 reduced). The 14th day would actually be a 7 Personal Day.

1 Personal Month or Day

This is a month or day for new beginnings. It is a great time to launch projects during your Personal Year. It is a time to get projects off the ground, be more independent and decisive. Use this time wisely. It is not a month or day to be lazy. You are planting seeds for the year.

2 Personal Month or Day

You are more sensitive now. You may need more comfort and healing. This is a time to be patient, diplomatic and persuasive. Resist the temptation to be too forceful. You will achieve more by cooperating and seeing the other person's point of view.

3 Personal Month or Day

This is a good period to network, be joyful, optimistic and creative. Use your creative talents now and expand your group of friends. Be careful that you don't become too scattered during this period; it is important to stay focused.

4 Personal Month or Day

During this time period you should concentrate on practical matters. It is a time to build structure. Take care of details and be methodical. It is a very good time period to add focus to your projects.

5 Personal Month or Day

This is a good period to make changes to your plans. It is an excellent period to move or change jobs. Keep in mind though the Personal Year is the strongest. Use this time period to refine your projects. This is an excellent period for travel. Expect the unexpected during this time period. Be prepared for change.

6 Personal Month or Day

This is a period to concentrate on the home and family. You will have more responsibility for others during this period. It is wise to accept any additional burdens without resentment. Your family and friends will need you now. The focus now is on counseling, teaching and healing others.

7 Personal Month or Day

This is a restful period. Try to balance your work with your personal life so that you have more time out for you. It is good period to reflect and analyze your plans. Make "you" the focus of your life during this period. Spend time alone so you can think your ideas through.

8 Personal Month or Day

This is a great month for implementing your plans. Go after what you want. Don't sit and wait. You will be asked to use your resources wisely. Pay attention to how you invest your money, time and energy. It can be a very good business period, but there can be expenses attached to this period.

9 Personal Month or Day

This is a period of closure. It is important to discard

what is not working or what you don't need. This is **not** a period to launch a new project. You are ending things now and should wait to a 1 cycle to get your new project off the ground.

෨ *Chapter 14* ൚

Random Numbers in Your Life

"If you would understand the invisible, look carefully at the visible."—Talmud

We are surrounded by numbers in our lives. I have many clients who ask me why certain numbers show up all the time. Sometimes they will show up in repetitive dreams. Other times you may consider them to be your lucky numbers. When you think of numbers, begin to think of them as qualities of vibrations. Think of them as specific types of energies. Just as I described in the beginning of this book; I spoke of numbers as having almost a personality. For example, the number 1 is a very independent, initiating number, the number 2 is a more sensitive, interdependent number, the number 3 is a creative energy, and so on.

If you have particular dreams pertaining to a set of numbers, go back and see what the qualities of those numbers are and what they total to. This can assist you in solving particular issues in your life. We are regularly drawn to certain numbers. Most prevalent is the number of the day we are born and our Learning Lesson or Life Path (the total of your date of birth). Some people will call this "their lucky number". Rather than being lucky, it is more of you or your essence. That is why you are so drawn to it.

Where You Live

There are particular numerical situations that affect your life. These are your house or apartment number and your automobile license plate. The house or apartment number is the vibration you are living in. The automobile license number is an indication of "how you want to be seen by others." *If your house number is one of your Karmic corrections (one of your missing numbers in your name), you will always be working on that Karma while you live in that house.* This shows you why you just love certain houses and others you wish you had never moved into. Remember, when you add up the numbers in a house or an apartment; always add the letter as a number. For instance, the letter "A" would be a 1 and "B" would be a 2 etc. *In an apartment building only use the apartment number and letters on your door.* The general building number has relevance, but not as much as your individual apartment number.

A Number 1 house wants its occupants to learn to be independent. It is a house in which you will be become more willful and be taught to stand on your own. Its occupants will be more driven to do their own thing. If there are only two people in this house, each will be more willful in doing his or her own endeavor. If you are living in a Number 1 house, your independence is stronger than partnership.

A Number 2 house desires peace and tranquility. It is the perfect home for a couple as the Number 2 always operates in pairs. If you live in a Number 2 house you can expect to learn compromise and patience while living at this location. You will feel more vulnerable and sensitive while in this space. If you live alone in this space, you might always feel you want to "be" with someone while at this address. It is a great space in which to write and use your creative talents. It encourages cooperation in the affairs that take place within its walls.

A Number 3 house is a highly creative place. It is a wonderful house for entertaining and for using any of your creative talents. Be careful in this space that you do not become scattered in too many pursuits. This type of home can encourage beauty in its occupants and a general pleasant atmosphere. The pitfall of this house is that its occupants become too complacent in their affairs. Concentrate on any specific creative talent while living in this house.

A Number 4 house requires that its occupants work and be practical. You will always find yourself working on the house. If you need to be more disciplined, this is the house that will help you. The only problem is that it can be overdone. You might have little rest in this house, as you will always be working. A 4 house might also box you in (the square), and as a result, you might find it more challenging to make change in your life while living at this address.

A Number 5 house is a very active house. People are usually coming and going. You will have people move in and move out. It is a great house for marketing and sales promotion, and an excellent house for a home office—particularly if you are marketing products and services. If you love serenity and seclusion, this is not your place. If you like a more lively lifestyle, this is it.

A Number 6 house is a great space for the family.

This is the nurturing space—the home, hearth, motherhood etc. It is a good home in which to raise children, garden, cook and experience endeavors having to do with the responsibilities of the family. It has a loving vibration to it. If you live in this type of energy, you might find yourself cooking and entertaining close family and friends. This house can be a safe haven in the community.

A Number 7 house is a wonderful place for those who need the privacy of their own world. This is a more retiring and restful space. It is not a home for entertaining, but could be the necessary retreat from the outside world. If you are in depression or feeling lonely, this might not be the best place to live. It doesn't encourage visitors. It can be a great place if you need a quiet environment in which to recover and contemplate. You will be very particular on whom you invite to visit you.

A Number 8 house is a great environment if you like big business and have large visions. An 8 house doesn't think small. It can have big expenses connected with its upkeep, but it is also a good environment for you to raise your standard of living. It wants accomplished people to live here. It wants you to make money and spend it on improving the house. You will push yourself to be more successful while living in this house. Since the number 8 has much Karma attached to it, you will have to use your resources very wisely. Watch your energy, time and money while living at this address.

A Number 9 house is wonderful if you can become a humanitarian and accept all others. It is a loving vibration. It is wonderful for the creative arts, and its occupants must be very forgiving. People from all walks of life should be welcomed here. You will want to beautify this home. There will be many people coming and going from this address. You will find yourself wanting to help the masses and doing some type of charity work while living in this home.

The Vehicle You Drive

I think it is very interesting to look at the vehicles people drive. Many times the vehicle is an extension of the person. The vehicle's license number will tell you a great deal about how the owner or driver of the vehicle wants you to see him or her. Even if the vehicle is beaten and battered, the owner will still want to be seen as the type of person that the license plate presents. It may surprise you. We unconsciously choose our license numbers—even the so-called "vanity" plates are chosen from our subconscious. Personally in my own life I have moved three times in the last 10 years. Each time I let the Motor Vehicle Department choose my license number. In fact, the moves were in two different states. Each of these three moves totaled to the same number. What appears to be a random drawing of numbers is actually your unconscious attracting the vibrations of those numbers and letters. To discover how you want to be seen with your license number, **add up the numbers and letters together.** See if they total a Master Number. What was the final single digit?

A Number 1 license number shows a driver who wants to be seen as independent, a leader, a self-starter and basically Number One. Even if the person doesn't exhibit any of these behaviors, this is how this person wants to be seen by others.

A Number 2 license number shows a driver who wants

to be seen as a peace- loving person, sensitive and cooperative. He or she wants to be viewed as a team player and one that can get along even though they may exhibit the opposite behavior.

A Number 3 license number shows a driver who wants to be seen as very pleasant, communicative and creative. This is sort of the "nice guy" number. "I want you to see me as the person who doesn't offend and always has something nice to say." This could or could not be the opposite of the person's behavior, but that is how he or she wants to be seen.

A Number 4 license number shows a driver who wants to be seen as the "salt of the earth," the hard worker, the disciplined person and someone who is organized and methodical. He or she wants to be seen as the person who gets the job done and the one you can depend upon. He or she wants to be seen as being very productive.

A Number 5 license number shows a driver who wants to be seen as being free. She wants to have the freedom to come and go and wants you to see her as someone who is a bit of a daredevil. Deep down he or she longs for freedom.

A Number 6 license number shows a driver who wants to be seen as being very responsible and caring. He wants you to think of him as being service oriented and very committed to home and community. This can be taken one step further where the person wants to be seen as the helper, healer, teacher and counselor.

A Number 7 license number shows a driver who wants to be seen as being very high minded and discerning. He or she wants to be seen as someone who thinks deeply, contemplates information, and has a great deal of knowledge. He or she wants to be seen as being smart with a very sound mind. This person may also want to be seen as being very spiritual.

A number 8 license number shows a driver who wants to be seen as being a leader, the boss. This individual wants to be seen as having power, success, money, etc. The person may have none of these qualities in his or her personality, but this is how he or she wants to be seen.

A Number 9 license number shows a driver who wants to be seen as the humanitarian—the generous Soul who helps others and wants to be seen as being kind and loving. This person also wants to be seen as being somewhat artistic with an eye for beauty.

ଭାଷ

৯০ *Chapter 15* ৫৩

Important to Keep in mind......

"You are never 'lucky,' you are 'blessed'."—Anonymous

I have taken the liberty to simplify multi-dimensional information that takes years of study. Sacred Geometry, Numerology and other Ancient Teachings have always been with us. Perhaps you will do more in-depth learning. Knowledge is very important. More important though, I believe, is how you use this knowledge. It is your own private search for understanding that will lead you to your authentic self. The best investment you will ever make is not in real estate, stocks or corporate ownership, but in yourself. Invest your energy, time and money in activities that enhance your Soul. By relying on your own intuition and trusting yourself, you will be guided to the wise teachers, the best books and the most enhancing experiences. Learn discernment. Question the teacher and the messenger. You can trust yourself.

1) Learn how to combine your Life Path or Learning Lesson with your Destiny. In order for a life to work well, these two must work together. Use your Life Path toward the direction of your Destiny.

2) If any of your Pinnacle numbers match one of your Karmic correction numbers, that period of time will be concentrated on balancing out that Karma.

3) If the **day** of birth (born on the 13th or 14th day, etc.) matches one of your Karmic numbers (numbers missing from your name), you are being assisted in balancing out that Karma. It is helpful to have your day of birth the same as this missing number. The day of birth also gives you quite a bit of the essence of that number. For instance, if you were born on the 8th day of the month, you would be carrying a good amount of power, authority and leadership. This may be helpful if you have Karma in the number eight.

4) If the total of your Soul Number (your vowels) matches your Life Path, you are repeating a plan over. It is very important to learn the lesson in this lifetime. Normally this is a very challenging incarnation. You will not be able to escape the program.

5) If your spouse or partner has the same Life Path as you, you have unfinished business with this person. It can be compared to two children forced to attend the same class and learn the same lesson. Watch out for competition that might arise as you learn your lesson.

6) If both partners are missing the number six in their birth names and have no other placement of six as one of their key numbers (Personality, Day of Birth, Life Path, Soul Urge or Destiny), it will be extremely challenging to hold the union together. Both have much to learn about commitment.

7) After you have completed seven of the seven-year cycles, or the age of 50, it is the time when you can begin to free yourself from the "shoulds" of your life. You again free yourself at the age of 57, after you have completed the cycle that begins at age 56. You are not held hostage to the false beliefs of others.

8) If you thought you would be retiring in a lifetime, think again. The Soul did not reincarnate to retire. You will be growing in awareness until you take your last breath.

9) Those Souls who carry Master Numbers must remember to choose partners who have at least one Master Number (11, 22, 33, 44 etc) in their plan. This is always the compound

number behind the single digit. Master Number (vibrations are very strong and partner best with others who have Master Numbers.)

10) In relationships, remember that the partner who has the same Destiny number as the other partner's Life Path/ Learning Lesson, is generally the teacher of that relationship (there are a few exceptions).

11) We routinely meet people and partner up with individuals who have been in our same Soul family. Some are very comfortable, others the opposite. It depends on the Karma you have with that person and the past-life memory.

12) Concentrate on this life. Stay grounded. You have decided to enter into this dense atmosphere of planet Earth to learn lessons using your free will and to experience emotional feelings. Stop trying to get out of it. Stay in the body.

13) All numbers are related. There are no good or bad numbers. You will routinely draw to you certain numbers (vibrations of those numbers) that are comfortable or helpful to your life plan (such as your house and car license numbers).

14) Release blame, denial, self-deception, irresponsibility, judgment and guilt. Focus on your own lessons, and stop trying to fix other people.

15) Choose to express yourself only in ways that will use your greater potential.

ଜୟ

๛ *Bibliography* ๙

Over the years of study, several authors have taught me to understand the Ancient wisdom. Many thanks to them. I recommend them to you to learn more about your Divine Design.

1. Javane, Faith and Bunker, Dusty: *Numerology and The Divine Triangle*, West Chester, PA, Para Books, 1980
2. Buess, Lynn: *Numerology for the New Age*, Sedona, AZ, Light Technology Publishing, 1978
3. Burke, June: *You Are Unique*, Totowa, NJ, Burke-Srour Publications, Inc., 1995
4. Decoz, Hans with Tom Monte: *Numerology Key to Your Inner Self*, Honesdale, PA, Paragon Press, 1994
5. Sargent, Denny: *The Tao of Birth Days*, Boston, MA, Tuttle Publishing, 2000
6. Head, Joseph and S.L. Cranston: *Reincarnation in World Thought*, New York, NY, The Julian Press, Inc., 1967
7. Campbell, Florence: *Your Days Are Numbered*, Marina del Rey, CA, DeVorss & Company, 1931
8. Schneider, Michael: *A Beginner's Guide to Constructing the Universe*, New York, NY, Harper Collins, 1995
9. Alder, Vera Stanley: *The Finding of the Third Eye*, New York, NY, Samuel Weiser, Inc., 1968

౩ Divine Design Worksheets ౭

YOUR DATE OF BIRTH TOTAL

_____

YOUR NAME AT BIRTH

_____

YOUR SOUL URGE/MOTIVATOR

_____

YOUR PERSONALITY

_____

YOUR DESTINY

_____

YOUR TIME FRAME:

Pinnacle 1_____

Pinnacle 2_____

Pinnacle 3_____

Pinnacle 4_____

YOUR PERSONAL YEAR

_____

❧ *Divine Design Worksheets* ☙

YOUR DATE OF BIRTH TOTAL

_____

YOUR NAME AT BIRTH

_____

YOUR SOUL URGE/MOTIVATOR

_____

YOUR PERSONALITY

_____

YOUR DESTINY

_____

YOUR TIME FRAME:

Pinnacle 1_____

Pinnacle 2_____

Pinnacle 3_____

Pinnacle 4_____

YOUR PERSONAL YEAR

_____

🔊 Divine Design Worksheets ca

YOUR DATE OF BIRTH TOTAL

_____

YOUR NAME AT BIRTH

_____

YOUR SOUL URGE/MOTIVATOR

_____

YOUR PERSONALITY

_____

YOUR DESTINY

_____

YOUR TIME FRAME:

Pinnacle 1_____

Pinnacle 2_____

Pinnacle 3_____

Pinnacle 4_____

YOUR PERSONAL YEAR

_____

❧ ABOUT THE AUTHOR ❧

Author and lecturer Gail Minogue helps people achieve insight into their life purpose, embrace change and become master builders of their lives. Numerous business and governmental organizations, educational and spiritual institutions, as well as individuals have experienced remarkable results from her extraordinary approach.

Gail has spent over twenty years studying Mystery School information including Sacred Geometry, Astrology and Hermetic Laws. With her unique background in the financial areas as a Commodities Broker for 14 years and a Managing Director in the Far East for a Swiss textile firm, Gail is no stranger to managing the ups and downs of life and its ever-changing cycles. During this time and with the help of enlightened teachers, vast libraries and soul-searching experiences, she learned the Universal Laws dealing with Order.

All of her studies added an inner dimension to her outstanding ability to facilitate personal growth. This highly specialized combination of practical "real world" experience and holistic inner teachings allows Gail to bridge the two worlds. She is dedicated to helping people recognize their true value and maximize their talents and skills. Gail travels worldwide with her workshops, lectures and guest appearances. She is the mother of four grown children and makes her home in Los Angeles.

For information regarding Gail's workshops, book, tapes or private consultations, you may contact the author by calling or writing:

Gail K. Minogue
19528 Ventura Blvd. #603
Tarzana, CA 91356
Phone: 800-600-0256
818-377-4533
e-mail: gail@gailminogue.com